Oxford First Dictionary

new edition

OXFORD

Compiled by Andrew Delahunty

OXFORD
UNIVERSITY PRESS

OXFORD
UNIVERSITY PRESS

Great Clarendon Street, Oxford OX2 6DP

Oxford University Press is a department of the University of Oxford.
It furthers the University's objective of excellence in research,
scholarship, and education by publishing worldwide in

Oxford   New York

Auckland   Cape Town   Dar es Salaam   Hong Kong   Karachi
Kuala Lumpur   Madrid   Melbourne   Mexico City   Nairobi
New Delhi   Shanghai   Taipei   Toronto

With offices in

Argentina   Austria   Brazil   Chile   Czech Republic   France   Greece
Guatemala   Hungary   Italy   Japan   Poland   Portugal   Singapore
South Korea   Switzerland   Thailand   Turkey   Ukraine   Vietnam

Oxford is a registered trade mark of Oxford University Press
in the UK and in certain other countries

© Oxford University Press 2011

Database right Oxford University Press (maker)

First published 2011
Based on text by Evelyn Goldsmith

Artwork by Dynamo Limited

British Library Cataloguing in Publication Data
Data available

ISBN hardback: 9780-19-273261-3
10 9 8 7 6 5

ISBN paperback: 9780-19-273262-0
10 9 8 7 6

Printed in Italy

TEACHERS
For inspirational support plus
free resources and eBooks
www.oxfordprimary.co.uk

PARENTS
Help your child's reading
with essential tips, phonics
support and free eBooks
www.oxfordowl.co.uk

The **Oxford First Dictionary** helps you enjoy and discover the meanings of words and shows you how to spell them. The words in this dictionary are in alphabetical order. When you want to look up a word, you look at the letter the word begins with. You can use the alphabet down the side of every page and the catch words at the top to guide you to the correct place. Can you find the word 'kangaroo'?

At the back of this book you can also explore more words to do with numbers, shapes, and time. Have fun with the word jokes — can you make up your own?

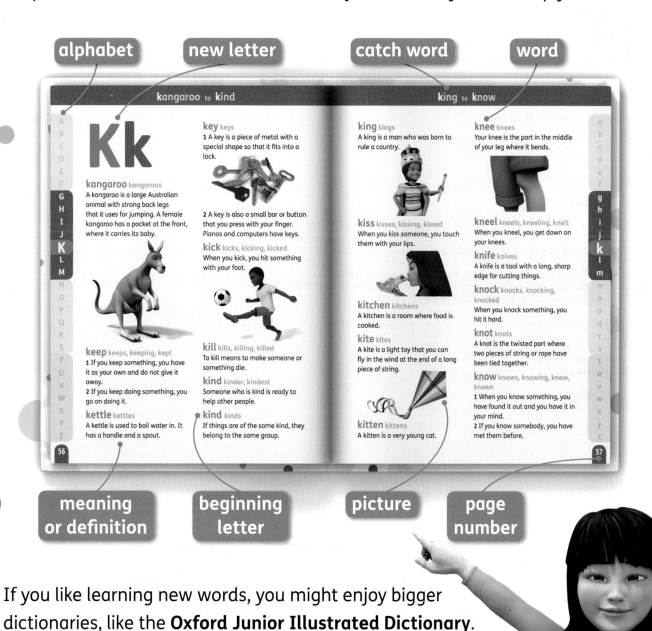

alphabet · new letter · catch word · word

meaning or definition · beginning letter · picture · page number

If you like learning new words, you might enjoy bigger dictionaries, like the **Oxford Junior Illustrated Dictionary**.

www.oxforddictionaries.com/schools

A B C D E F G H I J K L M N O P Q R S T U V W X Y Z

Aa

accident accidents
An accident is something nasty that was not meant to happen.

act acts, acting, acted
If you act, you pretend to be someone else in a play, show, or film.

add adds, adding, added
1 When you add something, you put it with something else.
2 When you add numbers, you work out how many you get when you put them together. So, three add two equals five.

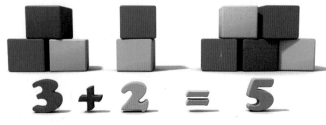

address addresses
Your address is the number of your house, and the name of the street and town where you live.

AIR MAIL

The Queen,
Buckingham Palace,
Buckingham Palace Road,
London UK
SW1A 1AA

adult adults
An adult is a person or animal that has grown up.

adventure adventures
An adventure is something exciting that happens to you.

aeroplane aeroplanes
An aeroplane is a flying machine with wings, and usually one or more engines.

afraid
Someone who is afraid thinks something bad might happen to them.

afternoon afternoons

The afternoon is the time from the middle of the day until about six o'clock.

age ages

The age of someone or something is how old they are.

agree agrees, agreeing, agreed

If you agree with someone, you think the same as they do.

air

Air is what everyone breathes. It is made of gases that we cannot see.

airport airports

An airport is a place where aeroplanes land and take off.

alive

A person, animal, or plant that is alive is living at the moment.

allow allows, allowing, allowed

If someone allows you to do something, they let you do it.

alone

If someone is alone, there is nobody with them.

alphabet alphabets

The alphabet is all the letters that are used in writing, put in a special order.

ambulance ambulances

An ambulance is a special van for taking people to hospital when they are ill or badly hurt.

angry angrier, angriest

If you are angry, you are not pleased at all with what someone has done or said.

a
b
c
d
e
f
g
h
i
j
k
l
m
n
o
p
q
r
s
t
u
v
w
x
y
z

animal animals

An animal is something that lives, can move about, and is not a plant. Elephants, parrots, bees, goldfish, and people are all animals.

ankle ankles

Your ankle is the part of your body where your leg joins your foot.

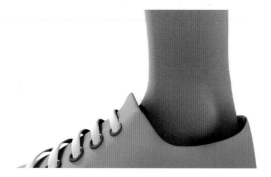

annoy annoys, annoying, annoyed

If someone annoys you, they make you angry.

answer answers, answering, answered

When you answer, you speak when someone calls you or asks you a question.

ant ants

An ant is a tiny insect. Ants live in large groups.

appear appears, appearing, appeared

If something appears, you can suddenly see it.

apple apples

An apple is a round fruit. Apples have green, red, or yellow skins.

argue argues, arguing, argued

When you argue with somebody, you talk about things you do not agree on.

arm arms

Your arm is the part of your body between your shoulder and your hand.

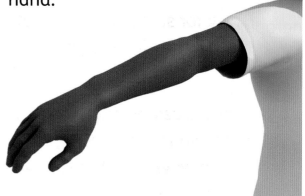

army armies

An army is a large group of soldiers who are trained to fight on land.

arrive arrives, arriving, arrived

When you arrive somewhere, you get there at the end of a journey.

arrow arrows

An arrow is a stick that you shoot from a bow.

art

Art is something special that someone has made, like a drawing or painting.

ask asks, asking, asked

1 When you ask a question, you are trying to find something out.
2 If you ask for something, you say you want it to be given to you.

asleep

When you are asleep, you are resting with your eyes closed, and you don't know what is going on around you.

astronaut astronauts

An astronaut is a person who travels in space.

attack attacks, attacking, attacked

If you attack someone, you try to hurt them.

attention

When you pay attention to somebody, you listen carefully and think about what they are saying.

audience audiences

An audience is a group of people who have come to a place to watch or listen to something.

aunt aunts

Your aunt is the sister of your mother or father, or the wife of your uncle.

author authors

An author is a person who writes a book or story.

A
B
C
D
E
F
G
H
I
J
K
L
M
N
O
P
Q
R
S
T
U
V
W
X
Y
Z

autumn autumns

Autumn is the part of the year when it gets colder, and leaves fall from the trees. It is the season between summer and winter.

awake

When you are awake, you are not asleep.

Bb

baby babies

A baby is a very young child.

back backs

1 The back of something is the part opposite the front.
2 Your back is the back part of your body.

bad worse, worst

Things that are bad are not good.

bag bags

A bag is used to hold or carry things.

bake bakes, baking, baked

When you bake something, you cook it in an oven.

balance balances, balancing, balanced

When you balance something, you keep it steady and stop it from falling over.

ball balls

A ball is round and is used in games and sports.

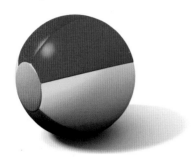

balloon balloons

A balloon is a rubber bag that you can blow into and make bigger.

banana bananas

A banana is a long, curved fruit with a thick, yellow skin.

band bands

1 A band is a group of people who play musical instruments together.
2 A band can also be a piece of material round something.

bank banks

1 A bank is the ground along the side of a river or lake.
2 A bank is also a place that looks after money for people.

bar bars

1 A bar is a long, thin piece of wood or metal.
2 A bar is also a block of chocolate or soap.

bare barer, barest

1 If part of someone's body is bare, it is not covered with anything.
2 A room or cupboard that is bare has nothing in it.

bark

Bark is the hard covering round the trunk and branches of a tree.

bark barks, barking, barked

When dogs bark, they make a sudden, loud sound.

basket baskets

A basket is for holding or carrying things. Baskets are made of things like straw, small branches, or wires.

a
b
c
d
e
f
g
h
i
j
k
l
m
n
o
p
q
r
s
t
u
v
w
x
y
z

9

A B **B** C D E F G H I J K L M N O P Q R S T U V W X Y Z

bat bats

1 A bat is a piece of wood for hitting the ball in a game.
2 A bat is also an animal that looks like a mouse with wings.

bath baths

A bath can be filled with water so that you can sit in it and wash yourself.

bathroom bathrooms

A bathroom is a room with a bath or shower.

battery batteries

A battery has electricity inside it. You put batteries in things like toys, watches, and radios to make them work.

beach beaches

A beach is land by the edge of the sea. It is usually covered with sand or small stones.

beak beaks

A beak is the hard part of a bird's mouth.

bear bears

A bear is a big, heavy animal with thick fur and sharp claws.

beard beards

A beard is the hair that grows on a man's chin and cheeks.

beat beats, beating, beat, beaten

1 If you beat someone in a race or game, you do better than them and win it.
2 To beat can also mean to keep hitting with a stick.

beautiful

You say something is beautiful if you enjoy looking at it or listening to it.

bed beds

A bed is a piece of furniture you sleep on.

bedroom bedrooms

A bedroom is a room you sleep in.

bee bees

A bee is an insect with wings. Bees make honey and live in a beehive.

beetle beetles

A beetle is an insect with hard wing-covers.

begin begins, beginning, began, begun

When you begin, you start something.

behave behaves, behaving, behaved

If someone tells you to behave, they want you to be good.

believe believes, believing, believed

If you believe something, you feel that it is true.

bell bells

A bell is a piece of metal that makes a ringing sound when you hit or shake it.

belong belongs, belonging, belonged

1 If something belongs to you, it is yours.
2 If something belongs somewhere, that is the right place for it.

belt belts

A belt is a band you wear round your waist.

bench benches

A bench is a long seat for more than one person.

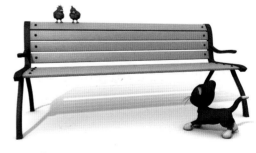

bend bends, bending, bent

If you bend something, you change its shape so it is no longer straight.

a
b
c
d
e
f
g
h
i
j
k
l
m
n
o
p
q
r
s
t
u
v
w
x
y
z

11

A B C D E F G H I J K L M N O P Q R S T U V W X Y Z

best

Something or somebody that is best is better than any of the others.

better

1 If someone can do something better than you, you are not as good at it as they are.
2 If one thing is better than another, it is more useful, or nearer to what you want.
3 If you have been ill but are feeling better, you are feeling well again.

bicycle bicycles

A bicycle is a machine that you can ride. Bicycles have two wheels and pedals which you turn with your feet.

big bigger, biggest

Somebody or something big is large.

bin bins

A bin is something to put things in. You can use bins to store things like bread or flour. Some bins are for rubbish.

bird birds

A bird is an animal that has wings, feathers, and a beak. Most birds can fly.

birthday birthdays

Your birthday is the day you were born.

biscuit biscuits

A biscuit is a kind of small, thin, dry cake.

bit bits

A bit is a tiny piece of something.

bite bites, biting, bit, bitten

If you bite something, you use your teeth to cut into it.

blanket blankets

A blanket is a thick cover for a bed.

blind

Someone who is blind cannot see at all.

block blocks

A block is a thick piece of something solid like wood or stone.

blood

Blood is the red liquid that moves round inside your body.

blow blows, blowing, blew, blown

1 When you blow, you make air come out of your mouth. You can blow candles out and blow up a balloon.
2 When the wind blows, it moves the air.

blunt blunter, bluntest

Something like a knife or a pencil that is blunt is not sharp.

boat boats

A boat floats and carries people or things on water.

body bodies

The body of a person or animal is the whole of them.

boil boils, boiling, boiled

1 When water boils, it is very hot and you can see bubbles and steam.
2 When you boil something, you cook it in boiling water.

bone bones

Your bones are the hard white parts inside your body.

bonfire bonfires

A bonfire is a large fire that someone lights outdoors.

book books

A book has pages fixed inside a cover. Books have writing or pictures in them.

boot boots

A boot is a kind of shoe that comes up above your ankle.

bored

If you are bored, you are not happy because you have nothing interesting to do.

boring

If something is boring, it is not interesting.

a
b
c
d
e
f
g
h
i
j
k
l
m
n
o
p
q
r
s
t
u
v
w
x
y
z

born

When a baby is born, it comes out of its mother's body.

borrow borrows, borrowing, borrowed

When you borrow something from somebody, you take it for a short time and promise to give it back later.

bottle bottles

A bottle is made to hold liquids. Bottles are made of glass or plastic.

bottom bottoms

1 The bottom of something is the lowest part of it.
2 Your bottom is the part of your body that you sit on.

bounce bounces, bouncing, bounced

When something bounces, it comes back again after hitting something else.

bow bows

1 A bow is a knot you use to tie a ribbon.

2 A bow is also a bent piece of wood used for shooting arrows.

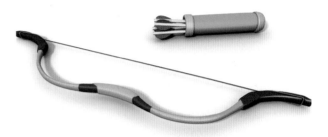

bow bows, bowing, bowed

If you bow, you bend over at the waist.

bowl bowls

A bowl is a kind of deep plate that is made to hold things like soup, fruit, or breakfast cereals.

box boxes

A box has straight sides and is made to hold things. Most boxes are made from cardboard, wood, or plastic.

boy boys

A boy is a male child or young adult.

brain brains

Your brain is inside your head. You use your brain for thinking and remembering.

branch branches

A branch grows out from the trunk of a tree.

brave braver, bravest

If you are brave, you show that you are not afraid.

bread

Bread is a food made by baking flour mixed with water.

break breaks, breaking, broke, broken

If something breaks, it goes into pieces or stops working.

breakfast breakfasts

Breakfast is the first meal after you wake up in the morning.

breathe breathes, breathing, breathed

When you breathe, you take air in through your nose or mouth and then let it out again.

brick bricks

A brick is a small block of baked clay. Bricks are used for building.

bridge bridges

A bridge goes over a river, railway, or road, so that people or traffic can get across, or under, or through.

bright brighter, brightest

1 Bright colours are strong and easy to see.
2 Bright lights shine strongly.

bring brings, bringing, brought

If you bring something, you carry it here.

broken

If something is broken, it is damaged and does not work any more.

broom brooms

A broom is a brush with a long handle. It is used for sweeping a floor or path.

a
b
c
d
e
f
g
h
i
j
k
l
m
n
o
p
q
r
s
t
u
v
w
x
y
z

A B C D E F G H I J K L M N O P Q R S T U V W X Y Z

brother brothers

Your brother is a boy who has the same parents as you do.

brush brushes

A brush has lots of short, stiff hairs, fixed into a handle made of wood or plastic. You use a hairbrush to make your hair tidy. You use a toothbrush to clean your teeth. You use a paintbrush to paint with.

bubble bubbles

A bubble is a small ball of soap or liquid with air inside.

bucket buckets

A bucket has a handle and is used to carry liquids or sand.

build builds, building, built

If you build something, you make it by putting different parts together.

building buildings

A building has walls and a roof. Houses, factories, and schools are buildings.

bulb bulbs

1 A bulb is the glass part of a lamp that gives light.

2 A bulb can also be the root of a flower. Daffodils and tulips grow from bulbs.

bull bulls

A bull is a large male animal of the cow family.

bump bumps

A bump is a round part that sticks out from something. If you knock your head, you sometimes get a bump on it.

burn burns, burning, burnt, burned

1 If something is burning, it is on fire.
2 If someone burns something, they damage it with fire or heat.

burst bursts, bursting, burst
When something bursts, it breaks open suddenly. Bags and balloons sometimes burst.

bus buses
Buses are big vehicles that can carry lots of people to and from places.

bush bushes
A bush is like a small tree, with lots of branches.

busy busier, busiest
1 Someone who is busy has a lot to do.
2 When a place is busy, there's a lot going on.

butter
Butter is a yellow food that is made from cream. You can spread it on bread or cook with it.

butterfly butterflies
A butterfly is an insect with four large wings.

button buttons
Buttons are small, round pieces that you fasten your clothes with. You push them through small holes in your clothes.

buy buys, buying, bought
When you buy something, you pay money to have it.

buzz buzzes, buzzing, buzzed
If something buzzes, it makes a humming sound like a bee makes.

Cc

cage cages
A cage is a box or room with bars. Pets like mice live in cages.

cake cakes
A cake is food made with flour, butter, eggs, and sugar. You bake a cake in the oven.

calculator calculators
A calculator is a machine that you use to do sums.

calendar calendars
A calendar is a list showing all the days, weeks, and months in a year.

calf calves
A calf is a young cow or bull.

call calls, calling, called
1 If you call someone, you speak loudly so that they will come to you.
2 If a person or thing is called something, that is their name.

camera cameras
You use a camera to take photos.

camp camps
A camp is a group of tents or huts where people live for a short time.

camp camps, camping, camped
If you go camping, you sleep in a tent.

can cans
A can is made of metal. You can buy food or drink in cans.

candle candles
A candle is a stick of wax with string through the middle. You can set the string on fire and it gives light.

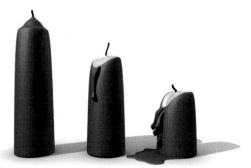

car cars

You can ride in a car. It has wheels and an engine to make it go.

card cards

1 A card has a picture on the front and a message inside. You send cards to people at special times.
2 Playing cards have numbers or pictures on them. You play games with them.
3 Card is thick, stiff paper.

cardboard

Cardboard is very thick, strong paper.

care cares, caring, cared

1 If you care for something, you look after it.
2 If you care about something, you think it matters.

careful

If you are careful, you think about what you are doing and try to do it without making mistakes.

carpet carpets

A carpet is a thick cover for the floor.

carry carries, carrying, carried

If you carry something, you take it from one place to another.

cartoon cartoons

1 A cartoon is a film that uses drawings instead of actors.
2 A cartoon is also a funny drawing.

castle castles

A castle is a large, strong building with very thick stone walls. Castles were built long ago to keep the people inside safe from their enemies.

cat cats

A cat is a furry animal. Small cats are often kept as pets. Large cats like lions and tigers live in the wild.

a
b
c
d
e
f
g
h
i
j
k
l
m
n
o
p
q
r
s
t
u
v
w
x
y
z

19

catch catches, catching, caught

1 When you catch something that is moving, you get hold of it. If someone throws a ball to you, you catch it.

2 If you catch a bus, you are on time to get on it.

3 If you catch an illness, you get it.

caterpillar caterpillars

A caterpillar is a long, creeping animal that will turn into a butterfly or moth.

cave caves

A cave is a big hole under the ground or inside a mountain.

CD CDs

CD is short for compact disc. CDs hold music or information. You play them on a CD player or computer.

ceiling ceilings

The ceiling in a room is the part of it above your head.

cereal cereals

A cereal is a kind of breakfast food that you eat with milk.

chain chains

A chain is a number of rings joined together in a line.

chair chairs

A chair is a seat with a back and sometimes arms, for one person.

chalk chalks

Chalks are pieces of soft rock that you write or draw with on a blackboard.

change changes, changing, changed

When things change, they become different.

change

Change is the money you get back when you have paid more than something costs.

chapter chapters
A chapter is a part of a book.

charge
Someone who is in charge of something makes sure that it is looked after.

chase chases, chasing, chased
When you chase somebody, you run after them and try to catch them.

cheap cheaper, cheapest
Something cheap does not cost very much.

cheek cheeks
Your cheeks are the soft parts on each side of your face.

cheer cheers, cheering, cheered
When people cheer, they shout to show they like something.

cheese
Cheese is a food. There are lots of different kinds of cheese, but they are all made from milk.

chew chews, chewing, chewed
When you chew food, you use your teeth to break it up into smaller pieces.

chick chicks
A chick is a baby bird.

chicken chickens
A chicken is a bird that farmers keep. Chickens lay eggs that we eat.

child children
A child is a young boy or girl.

chimney chimneys
A chimney is a long pipe that takes smoke from a fire up through the roof of a building.

chin chins
Your chin is the part of your face that is below your mouth.

chocolate chocolates
Chocolate is a sweet brown food or drink.

choose chooses, choosing, chose, chosen

If you choose something, you make up your mind which one you want.

chop chops, chopping, chopped

If you chop something, you cut it up with an axe or a knife.

circle circles

A circle is a round shape like a ring.

circus circuses

A circus is a show in a big tent that travels from place to place. You can see clowns at a circus, and sometimes animals that have been trained to do tricks.

city cities

A city is a very big town, like London or New York.

clap claps, clapping, clapped

If you clap, you hit your hands together to make a noise. People often clap to show they have enjoyed something.

class classes

A class is a group of pupils who learn together.

claw claws

A claw is the sharp, curved nail on the foot of an animal or bird.

clean cleaner, cleanest

Something that is clean has no dirty marks on it.

clean cleans, cleaning, cleaned

When you clean something, you get all the dirt off it. You clean your face with soap, and you clean your teeth with a toothbrush.

clear clearer, clearest

1 If something is clear, it is easy to see, hear, or understand.
2 If something is clear, there is nothing getting in the way. If a road is clear, there are no cars coming.
3 If something like glass, plastic, or water is clear, you can see through it.

clear clears, clearing, cleared

When you clear a place, you remove things or put them away.

clever cleverer, cleverest

Someone who is clever can learn and understand things easily.

cliff cliffs

A cliff is a hill with one side that goes straight down. Cliffs are often near the sea.

climb climbs, climbing, climbed

When you climb, you go up or down something high. You sometimes use your hands to help you, for example to climb a tree.

clock clocks

A clock is a machine that shows you what the time is.

close closer, closest

When something is close, it is near.

close closes, closing, closed

When you close something, you shut it.

cloth cloths

1 Cloth is material for making things like clothes and curtains.
2 A cloth is a piece of cloth for cleaning or covering something.

clothes

Clothes are the things that people wear.

cloud clouds

You can see clouds floating in the sky. They can be white or grey. Clouds are made of tiny drops of water that sometimes fall as rain.

clown clowns

A clown wears funny clothes, has a painted face, and does silly things to make people laugh.

coat coats

You put a coat on top of other clothes when you go outside. Coats have long sleeves.

a
b
c
d
e
f
g
h
i
j
k
l
m
n
o
p
q
r
s
t
u
v
w
x
y
z

coin coins

A coin is a piece of metal money.

cold colder, coldest

If you are cold, you feel that you want to put on warm clothes, or stand near something warm.

cold colds

A cold is an illness that makes you sneeze and your nose run.

collar collars

1 A collar is the part that goes round the neck of clothes like shirts and jackets.
2 A collar is also a band that goes round the neck of a dog or cat.

colour colours

Red, blue, and yellow are all colours. You can mix these together to get other colours.

come comes, coming, came, come

If you come to a place, you go towards it or arrive there.

comfortable

If something is comfortable, it feels good to be in or to wear. You can say that a chair or bed is comfortable, or a jumper or pair of shoes.

comic comics

A comic is a paper with stories told in pictures.

computer computers

A computer is a machine that stores information. Computers can also work things out, or help other machines to work.

control controls, controlling, controlled

If you control something, you are in charge of it and make it do what you want.

cook cooks, cooking, cooked

If someone cooks food, they get it ready to eat by heating it.

cooker cookers

A cooker is a machine for cooking food. It has an oven below for baking, and places on top for boiling or frying.

cool cooler, coolest

If something is cool, it feels quite cold but not too cold.

copy copies, copying, copied

If you copy something, you do it the same. So, if you copy a picture, you draw or paint a picture that looks just the same.

corner corners

A corner is the point where two sides, edges, or streets meet. A square has four corners.

cost costs, costing, cost

If something costs some money, that is how much you have to pay to buy it.

cough coughs, coughing, coughed

When you cough, you make a sudden loud noise with your throat.

count counts, counting, counted

1 When you count, you say numbers in order. Can you count up to 100?

2 To count also means to use numbers to find out how many people or things there are. Can you count how many words are explained on this page?

country countries

1 A country is a land with its own people and laws. France, the United States of America, and China are all countries.

2 The country is land with farms and villages away from towns.

cousin cousins

Your cousin is the son or daughter of your aunt or uncle.

cover covers, covering, covered

If you cover something, you put another thing over or round it.

cover covers

A cover is something that goes over or around something else. We put covers on cushions, books, and other things.

cow cows

A cow is a large female animal that gives milk.

crack cracks

A crack is a thin line on something where it has broken but not come to pieces.

a
b
c
d
e
f
g
h
i
j
k
l
m
n
o
p
q
r
s
t
u
v
w
x
y
z

cracker crackers

1 A cracker is a thin biscuit.

2 A cracker is also a paper tube which bangs when two people pull it. People often pull crackers at Christmas.

crane cranes

A crane is a tall machine that lifts very heavy things.

crash crashes, crashing, crashed

When something crashes, it falls or hits something else with a loud noise.

crash crashes

1 A crash is a very loud noise.

2 A crash is also a traffic accident.

crawl crawls, crawling, crawled

When you crawl, you move along on your hands and knees.

crayon crayons

A crayon is a coloured pencil often made of wax.

cream

Cream is the thick part of milk, often used in cakes and puddings.

creature creatures

A creature is any animal.

creep creeps, creeping, crept

1 If you creep somewhere, you walk very slowly and quietly so no one will hear you.

2 An animal that creeps moves along close to the ground.

crocodile crocodiles

A crocodile is a large animal that lives in rivers in some hot countries.

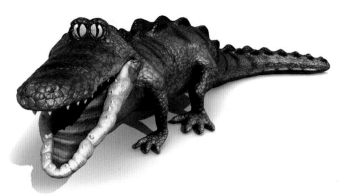

cross crosser, crossest

If you are cross, you feel annoyed about something.

cross crosses

A cross is a mark like this ✚ or this **X**.

cross crosses, crossing, crossed

If you cross something like a river or road, you go from one side to the other.

crowd crowds

A crowd is lots of people in one place.

crown crowns

A crown is a ring of gold and jewels that kings and queens wear on their heads.

crust crusts

A crust is the hard part on the outside of bread.

cry cries, crying, cried

When you cry, tears fall from your eyes. People cry when they are sad or hurt.

cry cries

A cry is a shout.

cuddle cuddles, cuddling, cuddled

If you cuddle someone, you hold them closely in your arms.

cup cups

People drink things like tea from a cup. A cup has a handle.

cupboard cupboards

A cupboard is a piece of furniture with a door at the front. You keep things in a cupboard.

curl curls

Curls are pieces of hair that grow or are twisted into rings.

curl curls, curling, curled

If you curl up, you sit or lie with your body bent round itself.

curtain curtains

A curtain is a piece of cloth that you pull across a window to cover it.

curved

Something that is curved is not straight.

cut cuts, cutting, cut

If you cut something, you use scissors or a knife.

cut cuts

A cut is an opening in your skin made by something sharp.

a
b
c
d
e
f
g
h
i
j
k
l
m
n
o
p
q
r
s
t
u
v
w
x
y
z

27

A B C D E F G H I J K L M N O P Q R S T U V W X Y Z

Dd

dad dads

Dad or daddy is what you call your father.

damage damages, damaging, damaged

If a person or thing damages something, they break or spoil it in some way.

damp damper, dampest

Something that is damp is a little bit wet.

dance dances, dancing, danced

When you dance, you move about in time to music.

danger dangers

If there is danger, something bad might happen.

dangerous

Something that is dangerous might hurt you.

dark darker, darkest

1 If it is dark, there is no light or not much light.
2 Dark hair is brown or black.

date dates

A date is the day, month, and sometimes the year when something happens.

daughter daughters

A person's daughter is their female child.

day days

1 The day is the time when it is light, from when the sun comes up to when the sun goes down.
2 A day is one of the twenty-four hours between one midnight and the next.

dead

If someone or something is dead, they are no longer living.

deaf deafer, deafest

Someone who is deaf cannot hear well. Some deaf people cannot hear at all.

decide decides, deciding, decided

When you decide, you make up your mind about something.

decorate decorates, decorating, decorated

1 When you decorate something, you make it look pretty.
2 When people decorate a room, they make it look fresh by painting it or putting paper on the walls.

deep deeper, deepest

Something is deep if it is a long way down to the bottom.

deer deer

A deer is a large animal that can run very fast. Male deer have big horns like branches on their heads, called antlers.

delicious

If something is delicious, it tastes or smells very nice.

dentist dentists

A dentist's job is to take care of people's teeth.

describe describes, describing, described

If you describe something, you say what it is like.

desert deserts

A desert is a hot, dry land where few plants can grow.

desk desks

A desk is a kind of table where you can read, write, draw, or use a computer.

destroy destroys, destroying, destroyed

If you destroy something, you damage it so much that it can no longer be used.

diamond diamonds

A diamond is a hard, shiny jewel that is clear like glass.

diary diaries

A diary is a book in which you can write down what happens each day.

dice dice

Dice are small cubes with spots on each side. You throw dice in some games.

dictionary dictionaries

A dictionary is a book where you can find out what words mean and how to spell them.

die dies, dying, died

When a person, animal, or plant dies, they stop living.

different

If something is different from something else, it is not the same.

difficult

Something that is difficult is not easy to do or understand.

dig digs, digging, dug

To dig means to move soil away to make a hole in the ground.

dinner dinners

Dinner is the main meal of the day.

dinosaur dinosaurs

A dinosaur is a large animal that lived millions of years ago.

direction directions

A direction is the way you are going or pointing.

dirt

Dirt is dust, mud, or earth.

dirty dirtier, dirtiest

Something that is dirty is covered with mud, food, or other marks.

disappear disappears, disappearing, disappeared

If something disappears, you cannot see it any longer.

disappointed

If you are disappointed, you feel sad because something you were hoping for did not happen.

discover discovers, discovering, discovered

When you discover something, you find out about it or see it for the first time.

disguise disguises

A disguise is something you wear so that people will not know who you are.

dish dishes

A dish is a bowl or plate for food.

disk disks

A disk is a thin, flat piece of plastic that you use in a computer to store information.

distance distances

The distance between two places or things is how far they are from each other.

dive dives, diving, dived

If you dive, you jump head first into water.

divide divides, dividing, divided

If you divide something, you make it into smaller pieces.

do does, doing, did, done

When you do something, you finish it or spend time on it.

doctor doctors

A doctor is someone whose job is to help people who are sick or hurt to get better.

dog dogs

A dog is an animal that people keep as a pet or to do work.

doll dolls

A doll is a toy that looks like a baby or a small person.

a
b
c
d
e
f
g
h
i
j
k
l
m
n
o
p
q
r
s
t
u
v
w
x
y
z

dolphin dolphins

A dolphin is an animal that lives in the sea. Dolphins are very clever and friendly.

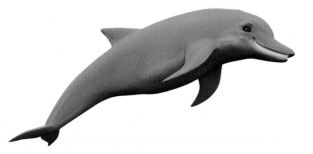

donkey donkeys

A donkey is an animal that looks like a small horse with long ears.

door doors

A door closes or opens the way into something like a house or a room.

drag drags, dragging, dragged

If you drag something, you pull it along the ground.

dragon dragons

In stories, a dragon is a monster that has wings and can breathe out fire.

draw draws, drawing, drew, drawn

When you draw, you make a picture with a pen, pencil, or crayon.

draw draws

If a game ends in a draw, both sides have the same score.

drawer drawers

A drawer is a box for keeping things in that slides in and out of a piece of furniture.

drawing drawings

A drawing is a picture made with a pen, pencil, or crayon.

dream dreams, dreaming, dreamt, dreamed

When you dream, you see and hear things in your mind while you are asleep.

dress dresses

A dress is something that girls and women wear. It is like a skirt and top in one.

dress dresses, dressing, dressed

When you dress or get dressed, you put your clothes on.

drink drinks, drinking, drank, drunk

When you drink, you swallow liquid.

drink drinks

A drink is a liquid that you swallow, like water, or milk, or fruit juice.

drip drips, dripping, dripped

When liquid drips, it falls in drops. Water sometimes drips from a tap.

drive drives, driving, drove, driven

When someone drives a car, a tractor, or a bus, they make it go where they want.

drop drops

A drop is a tiny bit of liquid.

drop drops, dropping, dropped

If you drop something, you let it fall.

drum drums

A drum is a musical instrument that you play by hitting it with a stick.

dry drier, driest

Something that is dry is not damp or wet.

duck ducks

A duck is a bird that lives near water and swims on the water.

dust

Dust is dry dirt like a powder.

Ee

ear ears
Your ears are the two parts of your body that you use for hearing.

early earlier, earliest
1 Early means near the beginning of something.
2 If someone is early, they arrive before you expect them.

earth
1 The Earth is the planet that we live on.
2 Earth is the soil or dirt that plants grow in.

easy easier, easiest
If something is easy, you can do it or understand it without any trouble.

eat eats, eating, ate, eaten
When you eat, you take food into your body.

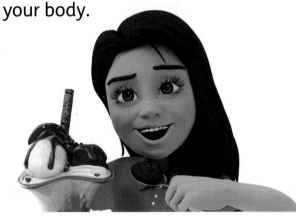

edge edges
An edge is the part along the end or side of something.

effort efforts
Effort is the hard work you put into something you are trying to do.

egg eggs
Baby birds, snakes, and insects live inside eggs until they are big enough to be born. Birds' eggs are oval, with a thin, hard shell.

elastic
When you pull elastic, it stretches. When you let it go, it goes back to its usual size.

elbow elbows

Your elbow is the part in the middle of your arm, where it bends.

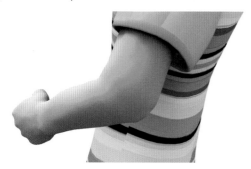

electricity

Electricity is power that moves along wires. We use electricity to give light and heat, and to make machines work.

elephant elephants

An elephant is a very large, grey animal with a very long nose, called a trunk, and big ears.

empty emptier, emptiest

Something that is empty has nothing in it.

end ends

The end is the last part of something.

end ends, ending, ended

If something ends, it finishes or stops.

enemy enemies

An enemy is a person who wants to hurt or fight you.

energy

1 If you have energy, you can move quickly and do a lot of things.
2 Energy is the power to make machines work.

engine engines

An engine is a machine that makes things move. Cars and trains have engines.

enjoy enjoys, enjoying, enjoyed

If you enjoy something, you like doing it.

enormous

Something enormous is very big.

envelope envelopes

An envelope is a paper cover for a letter.

environment environments

The environment is the air, land, and water that is all around us.

a
b
c
d
e
f
g
h
i
j
k
l
m
n
o
p
q
r
s
t
u
v
w
x
y
z

equal equals, equalling, equalled

If something equals something else, the two things are the same size or the same number.

equipment

Equipment is all the things you need for doing something.

escape escapes, escaping, escaped

If a person or animal escapes, they get away from something.

even

1 If a number is even, it can be divided by two, with nothing left over.

2 If two scores are even, they are the same.

3 If a path is even, it is flat and smooth.

evening evenings

The evening is the time at the end of the day when the sun sets, before people go to bed.

excellent

Excellent means very good.

excited

If you are excited, you are very happy about something and really looking forward to it.

excuse excuses

An excuse is what you say to explain why you have done something so that you will not get into trouble.

exercise exercises

1 Exercise is moving your body to keep fit.

2 An exercise is a piece of work you do to help you learn.

expect expects, expecting, expected

If you expect something, you think that it will happen.

expensive

Something expensive costs a lot of money.

explain explains, explaining, explained

If you explain something, you make it clear so that people can understand it.

explode explodes, exploding, exploded

When something explodes, it blows up with a very loud bang.

explore explores, exploring, explored

When you explore, you look carefully round a place for the first time.

extinct

If a kind of animal is extinct, there are none living any more. Dinosaurs have been extinct for millions of years.

extra

Extra means more than usual.

eye eyes

Your eyes are the two parts of your body that you use for seeing.

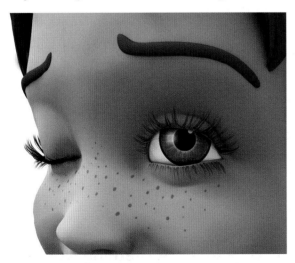

Ff

face faces

Your face is the front part of your head.

factory factories

A factory is a building where people and machines make a large number of things.

fair fairer, fairest

1 Something that is fair seems right because everyone is treated the same way.
2 Fair can mean light in colour.

fair fairs

Fairs are places where people can go to have fun. They are set up with rides for people to go on and games they can play to win prizes.

a b c d **e f** g h i j k l m n o p q r s t u v w x y z

fairy fairies

In stories, fairies are tiny people who have wings and can do magic.

fall falls, falling, fell, fallen

When something falls, it comes down suddenly.

family families

A family is made up of parents, children, and grandchildren.

famous

Famous people and things are very well known.

far farther, farthest

Something that is far away is a long way away.

farm farms

A farm is a piece of land for growing plants or keeping animals for food.

fast faster, fastest

Something that is fast can move quickly.

fasten fastens, fastening, fastened

If you fasten something, you do it up.

fat fatter, fattest

A person or animal that is fat has a very thick, round body.

fat fats

Fat is something like butter or oil that can be used in cooking.

father fathers

A father is a man who has a son or a daughter.

fault faults

If something bad is your fault, you made it happen.

favourite

Your favourite is the one you like best.

feast feasts

A feast is a special meal for a lot of people.

feather feathers

A feather is one of the soft, light things that cover a bird and help it to fly.

feed feeds, feeding, fed

If you feed a person or animal, you give them food.

feel feels, feeling, felt

1 If you feel something, you touch it to find out what it is like.
2 You can feel different ways at different times. So, if you feel excited or tired, that is how you are at the time.

female females

A female person or animal can have babies. Girls and women are female.

fence fences

A fence is a kind of wall made of wood or wire. People put fences around gardens and fields.

few fewer, fewest

Few means not many.

field fields

A field is a piece of land with a fence or hedge around it.

Farmers grow plants and keep animals in fields.

fierce fiercer, fiercest

A fierce animal looks angry and might attack you.

fight fights, fighting, fought

When people or animals fight, they try to hurt each other.

fill fills, filling, filled

If you fill something, you put so much into it that you cannot get any more in.

film films

A film is a story told in moving pictures. You watch a film at the cinema or on television.

fin fins

A fin is one of the thin, flat parts that stand out from a fish's body. Fins help fish to swim.

find finds, finding, found

1 When you find something that has been lost, you get it back.
2 If you find out about something, you learn about it.

fine finer, finest

1 Fine weather is dry and sunny.
2 If you say you are fine, you mean you are well and happy.

a
b
c
d
e
f
g
h
i
j
k
l
m
n
o
p
q
r
s
t
u
v
w
x
y
z

finger fingers

Your fingers are the five long, thin parts at the end of your hand.

finish finishes, finishing, finished

When you finish, you come to the end of something.

fire fires

1 Fire is the heat, flames, and bright light that come from something that is burning.
2 A fire is something that keeps people warm.

fire engine fire engines

A fire engine is a large truck that takes firefighters and their equipment to a fire.

firework fireworks

A firework is a paper tube filled with powder. When you light it, the firework makes a loud bang or burns with coloured lights.

first

If something or someone is first, they come before all the others.

fish fish or fishes

A fish is an animal that lives and breathes under water. Fish are covered with scales, and they have fins and a tail for swimming.

fish fishes, fishing, fished

If you fish, you try to catch fish.

fit fits, fitting, fitted

If something fits you, it is the right size and shape.

fix fixes, fixing, fixed

1 If you fix something that is broken, you mend it.
2 If you fix something somewhere, you join it firmly to something else.

fizzy fizzier, fizziest

A fizzy drink is one that is full of little bubbles.

flag flags

A flag is a piece of cloth with a pattern on it. Flags are usually fixed to a pole. Each country has its own flag.

flame flames
Flames are the orange, pointed parts you see rising up from a fire.

flash flashes
A flash is a sudden bright light.

flat flatter, flattest
Something that is flat does not slope or have any bumps. The top of a table is flat.

flat flats
A flat is a home. It is a set of rooms inside a house or big building.

flavour flavours
The flavour of food or drink is what it tastes like.

flipper flippers
The flippers on animals such as seals or penguins are the flat arms that they use for swimming.

float floats, floating, floated
1 If something floats, it stays on top of a liquid.
2 If something floats through the air, it moves along gently.

flock flocks
A flock is a group of birds or sheep.

floor floors
A floor is the part of a room or building that people walk on.

flour
Flour is a powder made from wheat that you use to make bread and cakes.

flow flows, flowing, flowed
To flow means to move along like water.

flower flowers
A flower is the part of a plant that makes seeds. Many flowers are brightly coloured.

fly flies, flying, flew, flown
1 When something flies, it moves through the air.
2 When people fly, they travel in an aeroplane.

fly flies
A fly is a small insect with one pair of wings.

fog

Fog is a thick cloud that is close to the ground and difficult to see through.

fold folds, folding, folded

If you fold something, you bend it so that one part goes over another.

follow follows, following, followed

If you follow someone, you go after them.

food

Food is anything that you eat to help you grow and be healthy.

foot feet

Your feet are the parts of your body at the end of your legs that you stand on.

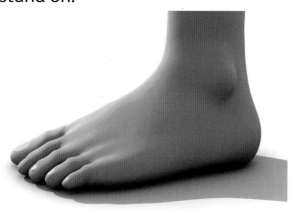

football footballs

1 Football is a game played by two teams who kick a ball and try to score goals.

2 A football is a large ball that you use to play football.

forest forests

A forest is a place where a lot of trees are growing together.

forget forgets, forgetting, forgot, forgotten

If you forget something, you do not remember it.

forgive forgives, forgiving, forgave, forgiven

If you forgive someone, you stop being angry with them.

fork forks

A fork is a tool with three or four thin pointed parts. People use small forks for eating and large forks for digging in the garden.

fox foxes

A fox is a wild animal that looks like a dog with a long furry tail.

frame frames

A frame is something that fits round the edge of a picture or window.

free freer, freest

1 If you are free, you can do what you like or go where you like.
2 Free things do not cost anything.

freeze freezes, freezing, froze, frozen

1 When water freezes, it changes into ice.
2 If you say you are freezing, you mean you are very cold.

fresh fresher, freshest

1 Fresh food has just been picked or made.
2 Fresh water is not salty.
3 Fresh air is clean and pure.

fridge fridges

A fridge is a metal cupboard that uses electricity to keep food cold and fresh.

friend friends

A friend is someone you know well and like and who likes you too.

friendly friendlier, friendliest

Someone who is friendly is kind and nice to be with.

frighten frightens, frightening, frightened

If something frightens a person or animal, it makes them feel afraid.

frog frogs

A frog is a small animal with a smooth, wet skin. Frogs live near water and have strong back legs for jumping.

front fronts

The front of anything is the side that people usually see first.

frown frowns, frowning, frowned

When you frown, you look cross or worried and lines come onto your forehead.

a
b
c
d
e
f
g
h
i
j
k
l
m
n
o
p
q
r
s
t
u
v
w
x
y
z

43

fruit fruits

Fruit is something like an apple, orange, or banana which grows on a bush or tree. Fruits have seeds in them.

fry fries, frying, fried

When you fry food, you cook it in hot oil or fat.

full fuller, fullest

If something is full, there is no more room in it.

fun

When you have fun, you enjoy yourself and feel happy.

funny funnier, funniest

1 If something is funny, it makes you laugh.
2 Something funny seems strange.

fur

Fur is the thick soft hair that covers some animals.

furniture

Furniture is all the big things like beds, tables, chairs, and cupboards that you need in a house.

furry

A furry animal is covered in thick, soft hair.

future

The future is the time that will come.

Gg

game games
A game is something you play that has rules. Football, chess, and hide-and-seek are games.

gap gaps
A gap is a space between two things.

garage garages
1 A garage is a building where you keep a car.
2 A garage is also a place that sells petrol or repairs cars.

garden gardens
A garden is a piece of ground where people can grow flowers and vegetables. Someone's garden is usually next to their house.

gas gases
A gas is anything like air, that is not solid or liquid. Some gases have strong smells. Some gases burn easily and are used for heating and cooking.

gate gates
A gate is a kind of door in a wall, fence, or hedge.

gentle gentler, gentlest
If you are gentle, you are kind, quiet, and careful.

get gets, getting, got
If you get something, you go to where it is and bring it back.

ghost ghosts
A ghost is the shape of a dead person that some people believe they have seen.

giant giants
A giant is a huge person in fairy stories.

a b c d e f **g** h i j k l m n o p q r s t u v w x y z

giraffe giraffes

A giraffe is a very tall animal with a long neck and long, thin legs.

girl girls

A girl is a female child or young adult.

give gives, giving, gave, given

If you give something to someone, you let them have it.

glass glasses

1 You can see through glass. It is used to make windows and bottles.
2 A glass is a kind of cup made of glass.

glasses

People wear glasses in front of their eyes to help them see better. Glasses are two pieces of glass or plastic in a frame.

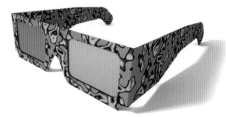

glove gloves

A glove is a covering for the hand with places for the thumb and each finger.

glue

Glue is a thick liquid used for sticking things together.

go goes, going, went, gone

If you go somewhere, you move from one place to another.

goal goals

1 A goal is the two posts that a ball must go between to score a point in games like football.
2 A goal is also a point that is scored when a ball goes into the goal.

goat goats

A goat is an animal with horns and sometimes a beard under its chin. Goats are sometimes kept for their milk.

gold

Gold is a shiny, yellow metal that is very valuable.

goldfish goldfish

A goldfish is a small orange fish often kept as a pet.

good better, best

1 If you say something is good, you like it.
2 Work that is good is done well.
3 If you are good, you behave well.
4 A good person is kind and caring.

goodbye

You say goodbye when you leave someone.

goose geese

A goose is a large bird with a long neck that lives near water.

grandfather grandfathers

Your grandfather is the father of your father or mother. You can also call him your grandpa.

grandmother grandmothers

Your grandmother is the mother of your father or mother. You can also call her your grandma.

grass

Grass is a green plant with thin leaves. There are usually lots of these plants growing close together in gardens and fields.

great

1 Great means very good.
2 Great also means large.

greedy greedier, greediest

Someone who is greedy wants more than their fair share of money or food.

ground

The ground is the earth or other surface that you walk on outside.

group groups

A group is a number of people or things that are all together or belong together.

A B C D E F **G** **H** I J K L M N O P Q R S T U V W X Y Z

grow grows, growing, grew, grown

When somebody or something grows, they get bigger.

guess guesses, guessing, guessed

When you guess, you give the answer to something without really knowing if it is right.

guitar guitars

A guitar is a musical instrument with strings. You play it with your fingers.

Hh

hair

Hair is the soft covering that grows on your head and body.

half halves

A half is one of two equal parts that something is divided into.

hand hands

Your hands are the parts of your body that you use for holding things. A hand has four fingers and a thumb.

handle handles

A handle is the part of something that you use to hold or carry it. Cups, baskets, and doors have handles.

hang hangs, hanging, hung
When you hang something, you fix the top of it to a hook or nail.

happy happier, happiest
When you are happy, you feel pleased about something.

hard harder, hardest
1 Something that is hard is not soft.
2 Something that is hard to do is not easy.

hat hats
A hat is something you wear on your head.

hate hates, hating, hated
If you hate someone or something, you feel very strongly that you do not like them or it.

have has, having, had
If you have something, it is with you or you own it.

hay
Hay is dry grass that is used to feed animals.

head heads
1 Your head is the part of your body that is above your neck and has your brain in it.

2 The head of something like a school is the person in charge.

healthy healthier, healthiest
1 If you feel healthy, you feel well and full of energy.
2 Healthy things are good for you.

hear hears, hearing, heard
When you hear something, your ears take in the sound it makes.

heart hearts
Your heart is a part of your body inside your chest. It sends blood around your body.

a
b
c
d
e
f
g
h
i
j
k
l
m
n
o
p
q
r
s
t
u
v
w
x
y
z

heavy heavier, heaviest

Something that is heavy is hard to lift or carry because it weighs a lot.

hedge hedges

A hedge is a kind of wall made by bushes growing close together.

helicopter helicopters

A helicopter is a vehicle that flies without wings. It has long parts, called blades, that spin round on top.

help helps, helping, helped

When you help somebody, you do something useful for them.

hen hens

A hen is a female chicken.

hide hides, hiding, hid, hidden

1 When you hide, you get into a place where no one can see you.
2 If you hide something, you put it into a place where no one can see it.

high higher, highest

1 Something like a wall or a mountain that is high goes up a long way.
2 If something is high in the air, it is a long way up.

hill hills

A hill is land that is higher than the land around it. Hills are smaller than mountains.

history

History is learning about what happened in the past.

hit hits, hitting, hit

If you hit something, you touch it hard.

hold holds, holding, held

1 If you hold something, you have it in your hands or arms.
2 To hold means to have room inside for something.

hole holes

A hole is a gap or opening in something.

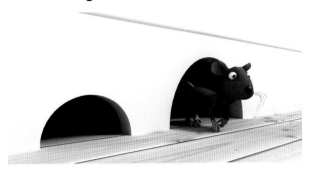

holiday holidays

A holiday is time off from school or work.

hollow

Something hollow has an empty space inside it.

home homes

A person's home is the place where they live.

honey

Honey is a sweet, sticky food made by bees.

hoof hoofs or hooves

A hoof is the hard part of a horse's foot. Cows and deer have hoofs, too.

hop hops, hopping, hopped

When you hop, you jump on one leg. Some animals and birds hop on two legs together.

hope hopes, hoping, hoped

When you hope that something is going to happen, you want it to happen.

horn horns

A horn is a kind of pointed bone that grows out of the heads of cows and other animals.

horse horses

A horse is an animal with hoofs that is used for riding and pulling things.

a
b
c
d
e
f
g
h
i
j
k
l
m
n
o
p
q
r
s
t
u
v
w
x
y
z

hospital hospitals
A hospital is a place where people who are ill or hurt are looked after.

hot hotter, hottest
1 When something is hot, it burns you if you touch it.
2 If you feel hot, you are too warm.

house houses
A house is a building where people live.

hug hugs, hugging, hugged
If you hug someone, you put your arms around them and hold them tightly.

huge
Something huge is very big.

human humans
A human is a man, woman, or child.

hungry hungrier, hungriest
If you are hungry, you want something to eat.

hunt hunts, hunting, hunted
1 To hunt means to go after a wild animal to kill it.
2 When you hunt for something, you look carefully for it.

hurry hurries, hurrying, hurried
When you hurry, you move or do something quickly.

hurt hurts, hurting, hurt
When something hurts, you feel pain there.

hutch hutches
A hutch is a kind of cage for a pet rabbit.

A B C D E F **G** **H** **I** J K L **M** N O P Q R S T U V W X Y Z

I i

ice

Ice is water that has frozen hard.

ice cream ice creams

Ice cream is a sweet, frozen food made from milk or cream.

idea ideas

An idea is something that you have thought of.

ill

Someone who is ill does not feel well.

illness illnesses

If you have an illness, you do not feel well.

immediately

If you do something immediately, you do it at once.

important

1 If something is important, it matters a lot and you must think about it carefully.
2 If someone is important, people take a lot of notice of what that person says and does.

impossible

If something is impossible, it cannot be done.

information

Information is what you can find out about something.

ink

Ink is the coloured liquid that is used for writing with a pen.

insect insects

An insect is a very small animal with six legs. Flies, ants, butterflies, and bees are all insects.

instructions

Instructions are words and pictures that tell people what to do.

a
b
c
d
e
f
g
h
i
j
k
l
m
n
o
p
q
r
s
t
u
v
w
x
y
z

instrument instruments

A musical instrument is something that you can use to make music.

interesting

If something is interesting, you want to spend time on it or want to learn more about it.

invent invents, inventing, invented

If you invent something new, you are the first person who thinks of how to make it.

invisible

Things that are invisible cannot be seen.

invite invites, inviting, invited

If you invite someone to a party, you ask them to come to it.

iron irons

An iron is a hot tool that you use to make clothes smooth and flat.

island islands

An island is a piece of land with water all round it.

Jj

jacket jackets

A jacket is a short coat.

jam jams

1 Jam is a food that is made by boiling fruit with sugar until it is thick.

2 A traffic jam is when there are too many cars on the road and nothing can move.

jar jars

Jars are usually made of glass. They hold things like jam.

jewel jewels

A jewel is a valuable and beautiful stone.

jigsaw jigsaws

A jigsaw is a puzzle made from a picture. When you fit the pieces together, you can see the picture.

job jobs

1 Someone's job is the work that they are paid to do.
2 A job is also something you have to do.

join joins, joining, joined

If you join two things, you put them together.

joke jokes

A joke is a short story or a riddle that makes people laugh.

Why is the letter 'E' lazy?

A: Because it is always in

journey journeys

A journey is the travelling that people do to get from one place to another.

jug jugs

A jug is used for holding and pouring liquids. It has a handle and a spout.

juice juices

Juice is the liquid that comes out of fruit.

jump jumps, jumping, jumped

When you jump, you go suddenly into the air with both feet off the ground.

jumper jumpers

A jumper is something that you wear on the top part of your body. Jumpers have long sleeves.

jungle jungles

A jungle is a thick forest in a warm, wet part of the world.

a
b
c
d
e
f
g
h
i
j
k
l
m
n
o
p
q
r
s
t
u
v
w
x
y
z

Kk

kangaroo kangaroos

A kangaroo is a large Australian animal with strong back legs that it uses for jumping. A female kangaroo has a pocket at the front, where it carries its baby.

keep keeps, keeping, kept

1 If you keep something, you have it as your own and do not give it away.
2 If you keep doing something, you go on doing it.

kettle kettles

A kettle is used to boil water in. It has a handle and a spout.

key keys

1 A key is a piece of metal with a special shape so that it fits into a lock.

2 A key is also a small bar or button that you press with your finger. Pianos and computers have keys.

kick kicks, kicking, kicked

When you kick, you hit something with your foot.

kill kills, killing, killed

To kill means to make someone or something die.

kind kinder, kindest

Someone who is kind is ready to help other people.

kind kinds

If things are of the same kind, they belong to the same group.

king kings
A king is a man who was born to rule a country.

kiss kisses, kissing, kissed
When you kiss someone, you touch them with your lips.

kitchen kitchens
A kitchen is a room where food is cooked.

kite kites
A kite is a light toy that you can fly in the wind at the end of a long piece of string.

kitten kittens
A kitten is a very young cat.

knee knees
Your knee is the part in the middle of your leg where it bends.

kneel kneels, kneeling, knelt
When you kneel, you get down on your knees.

knife knives
A knife is a tool with a long, sharp edge for cutting things.

knock knocks, knocking, knocked
When you knock something, you hit it hard.

knot knots
A knot is the twisted part where two pieces of string or rope have been tied together.

know knows, knowing, knew, known
1 When you know something, you have found it out and you have it in your mind.
2 If you know somebody, you have met them before.

a
b
c
d
e
f
g
h
i
j
k
l
m
n
o
p
q
r
s
t
u
v
w
x
y
z

57

Ll

lace laces

A lace is a string that is used to tie up a shoe.

ladder ladders

A ladder is two long bars with short bars between them. People use ladders for climbing up and down.

lady ladies

Lady is a polite word for a woman.

ladybird ladybirds

A ladybird is a small flying beetle. Most ladybirds are red with black spots.

lake lakes

A lake is a lot of water with land all round it.

lamb lambs

A lamb is a young sheep.

lamp lamps

A lamp gives light where you want it.

land

Land is all the parts of the earth's surface that are not covered with water.

land lands, landing, landed

When people land, they arrive by aeroplane or boat.

lane lanes

A lane is a narrow country road.

language languages

Language is the words that people use to speak or write to each other. There are many different languages spoken in the world.

large larger, largest

If a thing is large, it is bigger than other things.

last

The last thing is the one that comes at the end, after all the others.

late later, latest

1 If you are late, you arrive after people are expecting you.
2 Late also means near the end of a time. So, late afternoon is near the end of the afternoon.

laugh laughs, laughing, laughed

When you laugh, you make sounds to show you are happy or think something is funny.

law laws

A law is a rule that everyone in a country must keep.

lawn lawns

A lawn is the part of a garden that is covered with short grass.

lay lays, laying, laid

1 If you lay something down, you put it down carefully.
2 When you lay a table, you get it ready for a meal.
3 When a bird lays an egg, the egg comes out of the bird's body.

lazy lazier, laziest

Lazy people do not like working.

lead leads, leading, led

1 If you lead people, you go in front of them to show them where to go or what to do.
2 If you are leading in a race or game, you are winning it.

lead leads

A lead is a strap fixed to a dog's collar so that you can control it.

leader leaders

A leader is a person or animal that is in charge of a group.

leaf leaves

A leaf is one of the flat parts that grow on plants and trees. Most leaves are green.

learn learns, learning, learnt, learned

When you learn something, you get to know something you did not know before.

leather

Leather is a strong material made from the skins of animals. It is used to make things like bags, gloves, and shoes.

leave leaves, leaving, left

1 If you leave a place, you go away from it.

2 If you leave something somewhere, you let it stay there and do not take it with you.

left

Left is the side that is opposite to the right.

leg legs

1 Legs are the parts of the body that a person or animal uses for walking.

2 The legs of a table or chair are the parts that touch the floor.

lend lends, lending, lent

When somebody lends you something, they let you have it for a short time and you promise to give it back later.

lesson lessons

A lesson is the time when someone is teaching you something.

let lets, letting, let

If someone lets you do something, they say you may do it.

letter letters

1 A letter is one of the signs you use to write words. There are twenty-six letters in the alphabet.

2 A letter is also a message that you write to someone.

library libraries

A library is a place where a lot of books are kept. You can go to read them there or borrow them to read at home.

lick licks, licking, licked

When you lick something, you move your tongue over it.

lid lids

A lid is a top or cover for something like a box or a jar.

lie lies

A lie is something you say that you know is not true.

lie lies, lying, lay, lain

If you lie on something, you rest with your body flat.

lift lifts, lifting, lifted

If you lift something, you pick it up and move it upwards.

light lights

Light is what lets you see. It comes from the sun, flames, and lamps.

light lights, lighting, lit

If you light something, like a fire or a candle, you start it burning.

light lighter, lightest

1 Things that are light are easy to lift or carry.

2 Colours that are light are pale.

lightning

Lightning is the bright light that flashes in the sky during some storms.

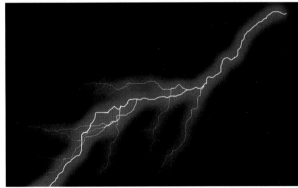

like

Something that is like something else is nearly the same.

like likes, liking, liked

If you like somebody or something, you think they are nice.

line lines

1 A line is a long, thin mark.

2 A line is also a row of people or things.

3 A railway line is the set of metal bars that a train moves on.

lion lions

A lion is a large wild cat. A male lion has a circle of long fur around its head.

lip lips

Your lips are the outside edges of your mouth.

liquid liquids

A liquid is anything that pours easily, like water, milk, or oil.

list lists

A list is a group of things or names that you write down one after the other.

listen listens, listening, listened

When you listen, you pay attention so that you can hear something.

A
B
C
D
E
F
G
H
I
J
K
L
M
N
O
P
Q
R
S
T
U
V
W
X
Y
Z

litter

Litter is paper, bottles, and other rubbish that people drop or leave behind.

little littler, littlest

1 Something that is little is smaller than other things like it.
2 If you have a little of something, you do not have very much.

live lives, living, lived

1 If something is living, it is alive.
2 If you live in a place, that is where your home is.

lizard lizards

A lizard is an animal with a long body, four legs, and a long tail.

lock locks

A lock is used to keep things like doors or cases shut. You cannot open a lock without the right key.

long longer, longest

1 Something that is long measures a lot from one end to the other.
2 Something that is long takes a lot of time.

look looks, looking, looked

1 When you look at something, you point your eyes at it so that you can see it.
2 If you look for something, you try to find it.

loose looser, loosest

If something is loose, it is not fixed firmly.

lorry lorries

A lorry is a big, open truck for taking heavy things by road.

lose loses, losing, lost

1 If you lose something, you cannot find it.

2 If you lose in a game or race, someone beats you.

lost
If you are lost, you do not know where you are.

lot lots
A lot is many or much of something.

loud louder, loudest
Something loud is easy to hear.

love loves, loving, loved
If you love someone, you like them very much.

low lower, lowest
If something is low, it is close to the ground.

lucky luckier, luckiest
If someone is lucky, good things seem to happen to them.

lunch lunches
Lunch is the meal that people eat in the middle of the day.

Mm

machine machines
A machine has parts that work together to do a job.

magazine magazines
A magazine is a kind of thin book that comes out every week or month. It has stories and pictures in it.

magic
1 In stories, people use magic to do impossible things.
2 Magic is also doing clever tricks that seem to be impossible.

magnet magnets
A magnet is a piece of metal that can make pieces of iron or steel stick to it.

main
The main thing is the most important or the biggest one.

a
b
c
d
e
f
g
h
i
j
k
l
m
n
o
p
q
r
s
t
u
v
w
x
y
z

make makes, making, made

1 If you make something, you get something new by putting other things together.

2 If you make a thing happen, it happens because of something you have said or done.

male males

A male person or animal cannot have babies. Boys and men are males.

man men

A man is a grown-up male person.

many

Many means a lot of something.

map maps

A map is a drawing of part of the world. Maps tell you where different places are and show you things like towns, roads, rivers, and mountains.

mark marks

A mark is a spot or line on a surface that spoils it.

marry marries, marrying, married

When two people marry, they become husband and wife.

mask masks

A mask is a cover that you can wear over your face. People wear masks to protect their faces or to change the way they look.

mat mats

A mat is a piece of thick material that covers part of the floor.

match matches

1 A match is a small, thin stick that makes a flame when it is rubbed on something rough.

2 A match is also a game played between two people or teams.

match matches, matching, matched

If one thing matches another, it is like it in some way.

material materials

Material is something that you can use to make things like clothes and curtains.

matter matters, mattering, mattered

If something matters, it is important.

meal meals

A meal is food that you sit down to eat. Breakfast, lunch, and dinner are all meals.

mean meaner, meanest

1 If something you do is mean, it is not kind to someone else.
2 Someone who is mean does not like spending money or sharing things.

mean means, meaning, meant

1 If someone tells you what a word means, they tell you how to use it.
2 If you mean to do something, you plan to do it.

measure measures, measuring, measured

When you measure something, you find out how big it is.

meat

Meat is food that comes from animals that have been killed.

medicine medicines

Medicine is a liquid or pills that a sick person takes to help them get better.

meet meets, meeting, met

When people meet, they come together.

melt melts, melting, melted

When something melts, it turns into a liquid as it gets hotter.

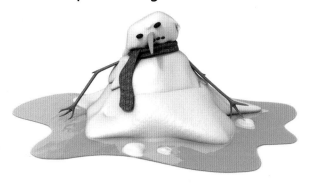

mend mends, mending, mended

When you mend something that is damaged, you put it right so that you can use it again.

mess

If something is in a mess, it is untidy or dirty.

a
b
c
d
e
f
g
h
i
j
k
l
m
n
o
p
q
r
s
t
u
v
w
x
y
z

A B C D E F **G H I J K L M** N O P Q R S T U V W X Y Z

message messages

You send a message when you want to tell someone something and you cannot speak to them yourself.

messy messier, messiest

If something is messy, it is untidy or dirty.

metal metals

Metal is hard and strong and melts when it is very hot. Gold, silver, and steel are all kinds of metal.

midday

Midday is twelve o'clock in the middle of the day.

middle

The middle of something is the part that is the same distance from all its sides.

midnight

Midnight is twelve o'clock at night.

milk

Milk is a white liquid that mothers and some female animals feed their babies with. People often drink cows' milk.

mind minds

Your mind is the part of you that thinks, feels, understands, and remembers.

mind minds, minding, minded

1 If you do not mind about something, you are not worried or upset about it.
2 If you mind something or somebody, you look after them for a short time.

mirror mirrors

A mirror is a piece of glass that you can see yourself in.

miss misses, missing, missed

1 If you try to hit something and you miss, you do not hit it.
2 If you miss a bus or train, you do not catch it.
3 If you miss somebody, you feel sad because they are not there with you.

mistake mistakes

A mistake is something that you did not get right.

mix mixes, mixing, mixed

When you mix things, you stir or shake them until they become one thing.

mixture mixtures

A mixture is made of different things mixed together.

model models

A model is a small copy of something.

mole moles

A mole is a small, furry animal that digs tunnels under the ground.

moment moments

A moment is a very small bit of time.

money

Money is the coins and paper notes that people use to buy things.

monkey monkeys

A monkey is an animal that lives in the trees in hot countries. It swings and climbs using its hands, feet, and long tail.

monster monsters

In stories, a monster is a huge, fierce animal.

month months

A month is part of a year. There are twelve months in a year.

moon moons

The moon moves round the Earth once every twenty-eight days. You can often see the moon shining in the sky at night.

morning mornings

The morning is the time from the beginning of the day until twelve o'clock noon. The sun rises in the morning.

mother mothers

A mother is a woman who has a son or a daughter.

motorbike motorbikes

A motorbike is a kind of heavy bicycle with an engine.

motorway motorways
A motorway is a very wide road, made so that traffic can move fast.

mountain mountains
A mountain is a very high hill.

mouse mice
1 A mouse is a very small animal with a long tail and a pointed nose.
2 A mouse is also a small box with buttons that you press to move things around on a computer.

mouth mouths
Your mouth is the part of your face that you open for speaking and eating.

move moves, moving, moved
1 If you move, you go from one place to another.
2 If you move something, you take it from one place to another.

mud
Mud is wet earth.

mug mugs
A mug is a large cup that does not need a saucer.

mum mums
Mum or mummy is what you call your mother.

muscle muscles
Muscles are the parts inside your body that help you move.

museum museums
A museum is a place where a lot of interesting things are kept for people to go and see.

mushroom mushrooms
A mushroom is a living thing that grows in the earth and looks like a little umbrella.

music
Music is the sounds that are made by someone singing, or playing a musical instrument.

Nn

nail nails

1 Your nails are the hard parts that cover the ends of your fingers and toes.

2 A nail is also a small piece of metal with a sharp point. Nails are used to join pieces of wood together.

name names

A name is what you call someone or something.

narrow narrower, narrowest

Something that is narrow does not measure very much from one side to the other.

nasty nastier, nastiest

1 Something that is nasty is not at all nice.

2 Someone who is nasty is not at all kind.

nature

Nature is everything in the world that has not been made by people. Mountains, rivers, animals, and plants are all part of nature.

naughty naughtier, naughtiest

Someone who is naughty behaves badly.

near nearer, nearest

If something is near, it is not far away.

neat neater, neatest

If something is neat, it is tidy and not in a mess.

neck necks

Your neck is the part of your body that joins your head to your shoulders.

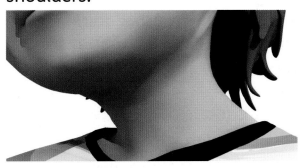

necklace necklaces

A necklace is a chain of jewels that someone wears round their neck.

a
b
c
d
e
f
g
h
i
j
k
l
m
n
o
p
q
r
s
t
u
v
w
x
y
z

69

A B C D E F G H I J K L M **N** O P Q R S T U V W X Y Z

need needs, needing, needed

If you need something, you must have it.

neighbour neighbours

A neighbour is someone who lives near to you.

nephew nephews

A person's nephew is the son of their brother or sister.

nervous

1 If you are nervous, you feel afraid and excited because of something you have to do.
2 A person or animal that is nervous is easily frightened.

nest nests

A nest is a home made by birds, mice, and some other animals for their babies.

net nets

A net is made of string tied together with spaces in between. Nets are used in games like football and basketball. They are also used to catch fish and other animals.

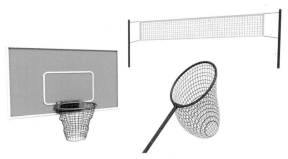

new newer, newest

1 Something that is new has just been bought or made.
2 New can mean different. So, if you move to a new house or start at a new school, it is a different one.

news

News is information about what has just happened.

newspaper newspapers

A newspaper is a number of large sheets of paper folded together. It tells you about things that are happening in the world. Most newspapers come out every day.

next

1 Next means the one coming after this one.
2 Next also means the one nearest to you.

nice nicer, nicest

If somebody or something is nice, you like them.

niece nieces

A person's niece is the daughter of their brother or sister.

night nights

Night is the time when it is dark, after the sun goes down.

nightdress nightdresses

A nightdress is a kind of long, loose dress that girls and women wear in bed.

nightmare nightmares

A nightmare is a frightening dream.

nod nods, nodding, nodded

When you nod, you move your head down and then up again quickly, to show that you agree.

noise noises

A noise is a loud sound that someone or something makes.

noisy noisier, noisiest

Something noisy makes a lot of loud sound.

noon

Noon is twelve o'clock in the middle of the day.

nose noses

Your nose is the part of your face that you use for breathing and smelling.

note notes

1 A note is a short letter.
2 A note is also one sound in music.

notice notices, noticing, noticed

If you notice something, you see it and think about it.

notice notices

A notice is a piece of paper or a sign that tells people something.

now

Now means at this time.

number numbers

Numbers tell you how many people or things there are. Numbers can be written as words one, two, three, or as signs 1, 2, 3.

nurse nurses

A nurse is someone whose job is to take care of people who are ill or hurt.

nut nuts

A nut is a kind of dry fruit that you can eat after you have taken off its hard shell.

Oo

oar oars

An oar is a long pole with a flat part at one end. You use oars to row a boat.

obey obeys, obeying, obeyed

When you obey someone, you do what they tell you.

ocean oceans

An ocean is a very big sea.

octopus octopuses

An octopus is a sea animal with eight long arms and a soft body.

odd odder, oddest

1 If something is odd, it seems strange.
2 An odd number cannot be divided by two without having something left over. 7, 13, and 25 are odd numbers.

offer offers, offering, offered

If you offer something, you ask someone if they would like it.

oil

Oil is a thick liquid. It can be burned to keep people warm, or put on machines to help them move easily. Some kinds of oil are used in cooking.

old older, oldest

1 Someone who is old was born a long time ago.
2 Something that is old was made a long time ago.
3 You say something is old if you have had it a long time.

open

When something is open, people or things can go into it or through it.

open opens, opening, opened

If you open something, you make it no longer shut or closed.

opposite opposites

The opposite of something is the thing that is as different from it as possible. Short is the opposite of tall.

opposite

If something is opposite something else, it is on the other side.

orange oranges

An orange is a round and sweet fruit with a thick peel.

order

Order is the way something is set out, one thing after another. The words in a dictionary are in alphabetical order.

order orders, ordering, ordered

1 If someone orders you to do something, they say you have to do it.
2 If someone orders something, they ask for something they are going to pay for, such as a meal.

other

Other means not this one.

outside

Outside means not in a building.

oven ovens

An oven is the space inside a cooker where food can be baked.

owl owls

An owl is a bird with a large, round head and large eyes. Owls hunt small animals at night.

own owns, owning, owned

1 If you own something, it is yours.
2 If you own up, you say that you were the one who did something.

Pp

paddle paddles, paddling, paddled

When you paddle, you walk about in water that is not very deep.

page pages

A page is one side of a piece of paper in a book.

pain pains

Pain is the feeling you have when part of your body hurts.

paint paints

Paint is a liquid that you put on the surface of something to colour it.

paint paints, painting, painted

1 If you paint a picture, you make a coloured picture with paints.
2 If someone paints something like a door, they put paint on to it.

painting paintings

A painting is a picture that someone has painted.

pair pairs

1 A pair is two people, two animals, or two things that belong together.
2 Things like trousers and scissors are also called a pair, because they have two parts joined together.

palace palaces

A palace is a very large house where people like kings and queens live.

pale paler, palest

Something that is pale in colour is almost white.

palm palms

Your palm is the inside of your hand between your fingers and your wrist.

pantomime pantomimes

A pantomime is a kind of play. It tells a fairy story, and has songs and jokes in it.

paper papers

1 Paper comes in very thin sheets and is used for things like making books, and for writing on and for wrapping things up.
2 Paper is also short for newspaper.

parachute parachutes

A parachute is used to help people float slowly down to the ground after jumping out of an aeroplane. It is made of a large piece of material that looks like a huge umbrella.

parcel parcels

A parcel is something that is wrapped up so that it can be posted or given to someone as a present.

parent parents

Your parents are your mother and your father.

park parks

A park is a large piece of land with grass and trees where anyone can walk or play.

park parks, parking, parked

When people park a car, they leave it somewhere for a short time.

parrot parrots

A parrot is a bird with brightly coloured feathers and a large, curved beak.

part parts

A part is anything that belongs to something bigger.

party parties

A party is when a group of people come together to enjoy themselves.

pass passes, passing, passed

1 If you pass something, you go by it without stopping.
2 If you pass something to someone, you give it to them with your hand.

passenger passengers

A passenger is anyone travelling in a car, bus, train, ship, or aeroplane.

past

The past is the time before now.

pasta

Pasta is food made from flour, eggs, and water, that is made into shapes. You cook pasta in boiling water.

paste

Paste is a thick, wet mixture that you can use to stick paper to things.

path paths

A path is a narrow way that you can go along.

patient

If you are patient, you can wait for a long time, or do something difficult, without getting angry.

patient patients

A patient is someone who is ill and is being cared for by a doctor.

pattern patterns

The pattern on a piece of material or a picture is the set of lines, shapes, and colours that appear over and over again on it.

paw paws

A paw is an animal's foot.

pay pays, paying, paid

To pay means to give money for work or for things you have bought.

pebble pebbles

A pebble is a small, smooth stone you find on the beach.

pedal pedals

A pedal is a part that you press with your foot to make something work. A bicycle has two pedals.

peel

Peel is the skin on some fruit and vegetables.

pen pens

A pen is something you use to write with in ink.

pencil pencils

A pencil is a long, thin stick with black or a colour right through the middle. You use a pencil for writing or drawing.

penguin penguins

A penguin is a black and white bird that usually lives in very cold places. Penguins cannot fly but they are good at swimming.

people

People are men, women, and children.

pepper

Pepper is a powder that you add to food to give it a strong taste.

person people

A person is a man, woman, or child.

pet pets

A pet is a tame animal that you keep in your home. Cats and dogs are often kept as pets.

petal petals

A petal is a coloured part of a flower.

phone phones

Phone is short for telephone.

photo photos

A photo is a picture taken with a camera. Photo is short for photograph.

a b c d e f g h i j k l m n o **p** q r s t u v w x y z

77

piano pianos

A piano is a large musical instrument. It has black and white keys that you press down with your fingers.

pick picks, picking, picked

1 If you pick somebody or something, you decide which one you want.
2 If you pick a thing up, you lift it.
3 If you pick flowers, fruit, or vegetables, you take them from where they are growing.

picnic picnics

A picnic is a meal you eat outdoors.

picture pictures

A picture is a painting, drawing, or photograph.

piece pieces

A piece of something is part of it.

pig pigs

A pig is an animal that is kept on a farm for its meat. Pigs have short, flat noses, called snouts, and curly tails.

pile piles

A pile is a number of things put on top of one another.

pill pills

A pill is a small, round piece of medicine that can be swallowed whole.

pillow pillows

A pillow is something soft that you rest your head on in bed.

pilot pilots

A pilot is a person who flies an aeroplane.

pin pins

A pin is a short, thin piece of metal with a sharp point at one end. You use pins to hold pieces of paper or cloth together.

pipe pipes

A pipe is a long, thin tube that carries gas or water.

pirate pirates

A pirate is a sailor who attacks other ships at sea and steals things from them.

pizza pizzas

A pizza is a large, flat kind of bread covered with cheese, tomatoes, and other foods. You bake pizza quickly in a very hot oven.

place places

A place is where something is or where it belongs.

plain plainer, plainest

Something that is plain does not have a pattern on it.

plan plans, planning, planned

When you plan something, you decide what is going to be done.

plane planes

Plane is short for aeroplane.

planet planets

A planet is any of the worlds in space that move around a star. The Earth, Mars, and Saturn are some of the planets which go around the Sun.

plant plants

A plant is anything that grows out of the ground. Trees, bushes, and flowers are all plants.

plaster plasters

A plaster is a piece of sticky material for covering cuts.

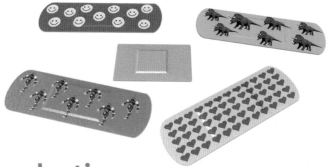

plastic

Plastic is light and strong. It is used to make bottles, bowls, buckets, toys, and many other things.

plate plates

A plate is a flat dish that you put food on.

play plays, playing, played

1 When you play, you do something for fun.
2 When you play a sport or game, you spend time trying to win it.
3 If you play a musical instrument, you make music with it.

playground playgrounds

A playground is a place outside where children can play.

a b c d e f g h i j k l m n o **p** q r s t u v w x y z

79

please pleases, pleasing, pleased

1 If you are pleased about something, it makes you feel happy.
2 You say please when you ask for something.

plenty

If there is plenty of something, there is more than you need.

pocket pockets

A pocket is a part of something you wear. It is like a small bag and is for keeping things in.

poem poems

A poem is a piece of writing that is written in short lines. The words at the end of the lines often rhyme.

point points

1 A point is the sharp end of things like pins and pencils.
2 A point is also part of the score in a game.

point points, pointing, pointed

When you point, you show where something is by holding out your finger towards it.

pointed

Something pointed has a sharp point at the end.

police

The police are the people whose job is to see that no one breaks the law.

polite politer, politest

Someone who is polite is well behaved.

pond ponds

A pond is a small lake.

pony ponies

A pony is a small horse.

poor poorer, poorest

Someone who is poor does not have much money.

possible

If something is possible, it can happen or be done.

post posts

1 A post is a tall, thick piece of wood or metal fixed in the ground.
2 The post is the letters or parcels that come to your home.

post posts, posting, posted

If you post something like a letter, you send it in the post.

poster posters

A poster is a large picture or notice for everyone to read.

pour pours, pouring, poured
When you pour a liquid, you make it run out of something like a bottle or jug.

powder powders
Powder is something that is made up of very tiny pieces, like dust or flour.

power
The power of something is how strong it is.

practise practises, practising, practised
When you practise something, you keep doing it so that you get better at it.

present presents
1 A present is something special you give to someone.
2 The present is the time right now.

press presses, pressing, pressed
When you press something, you push hard on it.

pretend pretends, pretending, pretended
When you pretend, you act as though something is true when it is not really.

pretty prettier, prettiest
Pretty means nice to look at.

price prices
The price of something is how much money you have to pay to buy it.

prince princes
A prince is the son of a king or queen.

princess princesses
1 A princess is the daughter of a king or queen.
2 The wife of a prince is also called a princess.

prison prisons
A prison is a place where people are kept because they have broken the law.

a
b
c
d
e
f
g
h
i
j
k
l
m
n
o
p
q
r
s
t
u
v
w
x
y
z

prize prizes

A prize is something you get for winning or for doing something well.

problem problems

A problem is hard to understand or do anything about.

programme programmes

A programme is a show on radio or television.

project projects

When you do a project, you find out as much as you can about something and then write about it.

promise promises, promising, promised

When you promise, you say you will really do or not do something.

protect protects, protecting, protected

If someone or something protects you, they keep you safe and stop you from being hurt.

proud prouder, proudest

If you feel proud, you are very pleased because you or someone close to you has done well.

pudding puddings

A pudding is something sweet that you eat at the end of a meal.

puddle puddles

A puddle is a small pool of water.

pull pulls, pulling, pulled

When you pull something, you get hold of it and make it come towards you.

pupil pupils

1 A pupil is someone who is being taught something.
2 Your pupils are the black spots in the middle of your eyes.

puppet puppet

A puppet is a kind of doll which can be made to move. Some puppets are put on like gloves, others are moved with strings from above.

puppy puppies

A puppy is a young dog.

pure purer, purest

Something that is pure does not have anything else mixed with it.

purse purses

A purse is a small bag for carrying money.

push pushes, pushing, pushed

When you push something, you use your hands to move it away from you.

put puts, putting, put

When you put something somewhere, you move it there or leave it there.

puzzle puzzles

A puzzle is a game or a question that is hard to work out.

pyjamas

Pyjamas are a pair of trousers and a loose jacket that you wear in bed.

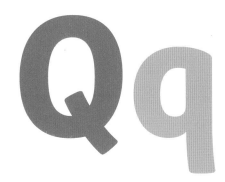

Qq

quack quacks, quacking, quacked

When a duck quacks, it makes a noise through its beak.

quarrel quarrels, quarrelling, quarrelled

When people quarrel, they talk in an angry way and sometimes fight.

queen queens

1 A queen is a woman who was born to rule a country.
2 A king's wife is also called a queen.

question questions

A question is something you ask when you want to find something out.

queue queues

A queue is a line of people waiting for something.

quick quicker, quickest

1 Something quick is done in a short time.
2 To be quick means to move fast.

quiet quieter, quietest

If someone or something is quiet, they make very little noise, or no noise at all.

quiz quizzes

A quiz is a kind of game or test. People try to answer questions to show how much they know.

Rr

rabbit rabbits

A rabbit is a small, furry animal with long ears. Rabbits live in holes in the ground.

race races

A race is a way of finding out who is the fastest.

radiator radiators

A radiator is made of metal, and is filled with hot water to heat a room.

radio radios

A radio is a machine that picks up sounds sent through the air. You can listen to music, programmes, or messages on a radio.

railway railways

A railway is a set of metal bars for trains to run on.

rain

Rain is water that falls from the sky in drops.

rainbow rainbows

A rainbow is the band of different colours that you can see in the sky when the sun shines through rain.

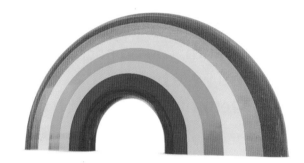

rare rarer, rarest

Something that is rare is not often found, or does not often happen.

rat rats

A rat looks like a mouse, but is larger.

raw

Raw food is not cooked.

reach reaches, reaching, reached

1 To reach something means to stretch out your hand to touch it.
2 To reach a place means to arrive there.

read reads, reading, read

When you read, you can understand words that are written down.

ready

If you are ready, you can do something at once.

real

1 Something that is real is not a copy.
2 Real also means true and not made up.

record records

A record is the best that has been done so far.

record records, recording, recorded

When you record something, you write it down or put it on tape or a CD.

recorder recorders

A recorder is a musical instrument. You play it by blowing into one end and covering holes with your fingers.

reflection reflections

A reflection is what you see in a mirror, or in anything shiny.

a b c d e f g h i j k l m n o p q **r** s t u v w x y z

remember remembers, remembering, remembered

To remember means to bring something back into your mind when you want to.

remind reminds, reminding, reminded

If you remind somebody of something, you help them to remember it.

remove removes, removing, removed

If you remove something, you take it away.

repair repairs, repairing, repaired

When someone repairs something, they put it right so that it works again.

reply replies, replying, replied

When you reply, you give an answer.

rescue rescues, rescuing, rescued

If you rescue somebody, you save them from danger.

rest rests, resting, rested

When you rest, you lie down or sit quietly.

rest

The rest of something is the part that is left.

return returns, returning, returned

1 If you return, you go back to where you were before.
2 If you return something, you give it back.

reward rewards

A reward is given to you for something good that you have done.

rhinoceros rhinoceroses

A rhinoceros is a very large, heavy animal with thick skin. It can have one or two horns on its nose.

rhyme rhymes, rhyming, rhymed

Words that rhyme have the same sound at the end, like bat and cat.

A B C D E F G H I J K L M N O P Q R S T U V W X Y Z

ribbon ribbons

A ribbon is a long, narrow piece of coloured material used to tie round hair or presents.

rice

Rice is a white food that comes from the seeds of a kind of grass. Rice is the main food for many people in the world.

rich richer, richest

People who are rich have a lot of money.

riddle riddles

A riddle is a kind of question that has a funny or clever answer.

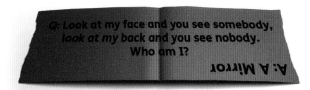

Q: Look at my face and you see somebody, look at my back and you see nobody. Who am I?

A: A Mirror

ride rides, riding, rode, ridden

1 When you ride a bicycle or a horse, you sit on it as it goes along.
2 When you ride in something like a car or train, you travel in it.

right

If something is right, there are no mistakes in it or it is as it should be.

right

Right is the side that is opposite the left.

ring rings

1 A ring is a circle.
2 A ring can be a circle of thin metal that you wear on your finger.
3 A ring is also the sound a bell makes.

ring rings, ringing, rang, rung

When something rings, it makes the sound of a bell.

rise rises, rising, rose, risen

When something rises, it goes upwards. When the sun rises, it moves up into the sky.

river rivers

A river is water that flows across the land to the sea or to a lake.

road roads

A road is a way between places, made for cars and buses, bicycles, and trucks.

roar roars, roaring, roared

To roar is to make a loud, deep sound. Lions roar.

a
b
c
d
e
f
g
h
i
j
k
l
m
n
o
p
q
r
s
t
u
v
w
x
y
z

87

robot robots

A robot is a machine that can move and do some jobs that people find boring.

rock rocks

Rock is the hard, stony part found in earth. A rock is a piece of this.

rock rocks, rocking, rocked

If something rocks, it moves gently from side to side.

rocket rockets

A rocket is a vehicle that can go very fast into space. Hot gases come out quickly from the end of the rocket and move it upwards.

roll rolls

1 A roll of something like tape or paper is a very long piece of it wrapped round and round lots of times.

2 A roll is also a small, round piece of bread made for one person.

roll rolls, rolling, rolled

When something rolls, it moves along on wheels or by turning over and over like a ball.

roof roofs

A roof is the part that covers the top of a building or vehicle.

room rooms

A room is one of the spaces with walls round it in a building. A room has a floor, ceiling, and its own door.

root roots

A root is the part of a plant that grows under the ground.

rope ropes

Rope is a long piece of thick, strong string.

rose roses

A rose is a beautiful flower with a sweet smell.

rough rougher, roughest

1 Something that is rough is not smooth.
2 If people are rough, they are not gentle.

round rounder, roundest

Something round has a shape like a circle or a ball.

row rows

A row is a line of people or things.

row rows, rowing, rowed

When you row, you use oars to make a boat move through water.

rub rubs, rubbing, rubbed

If you rub something, you press your hand on it and move it backwards and forwards.

rubber rubbers

1 Rubber is strong and stretches, bends, and bounces. It is used to make things like car tyres.
2 A rubber is a small piece of soft rubber that you use to rub out pencil marks.

rubbish

Rubbish is things that are not wanted, like empty cans and waste paper.

rude ruder, rudest

Someone who is rude behaves badly and is not polite.

rule rules, ruling, ruled

Someone who rules a country is in charge of it and the people who live there.

a
b
c
d
e
f
g
h
i
j
k
l
m
n
o
p
q
r
s
t
u
v
w
x
y
z

rule rules

Rules tell you what you can and cannot do. Games have rules, and places like schools have rules too.

ruler rulers

1 A ruler is a flat, straight piece of wood or plastic used for measuring and drawing straight lines.
2 A ruler is also someone who rules a country.

run runs, running, ran, run

When you run, you use your legs to move quickly.

Ss

sad sadder, saddest

If you are sad, you do not feel happy.

safe safer, safest

If someone is safe, they are free from danger.

sail sails

A sail is a large piece of strong cloth joined to a boat. The wind blows into the sail and makes the boat move.

sail sails, sailing, sailed

To sail means to travel in a boat.

A B C D E F G H I J K L M N O P Q R S T U V W X Y Z

salad salads
Salad is a mixture of raw vegetables, usually eaten as part of a meal.

salt
Salt is a white powder you put on food to give it flavour.

same
If two things are the same, they are like each other in every way.

sand
Sand is powder made up of tiny bits of rock. Sand covers deserts and the land next to the sea.

sandal sandals
A sandal is an open shoe with straps that go over your foot. People wear sandals in warm weather.

sandwich sandwiches
A sandwich is two slices of bread with another food between them.

saucer saucers
A saucer is a small plate for putting a cup on.

sausage sausages
A sausage is made of tiny pieces of meat put into a thin skin.

save saves, saving, saved
1 If you save something, such as money, you keep it so that you can use it later.
2 To save someone means to make them safe from danger.

saw saws
A saw is a tool that has a row of sharp teeth on one edge. Saws are used for cutting wood.

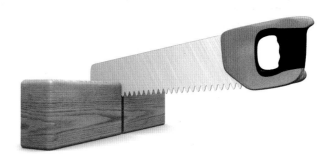

say says, saying, said
When you say something, you use your voice to make words.

scale scales
A scale is one of the small, thin pieces of hard skin that cover fish and snakes.

scales

Scales are used to find out how heavy things are.

scared

Someone who is scared feels afraid.

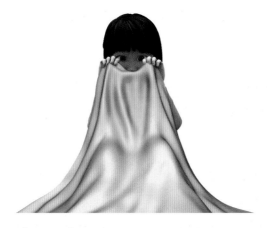

school schools

School is the place where children go to learn.

science sciences

Science is finding out about things that happen in the world around us. We do this by measuring things and by doing tests called experiments.

scissors

A pair of scissors is a tool for cutting paper or cloth. It has two long, sharp parts joined in the middle.

score scores, scoring, scored

To score means to get a goal or a point in a game.

score scores

The score is the number of points or goals each side has in a game.

scratch scratches, scratching, scratched

1 If you scratch something, you damage it by moving something sharp over it.
2 To scratch also means to rub your skin with your fingernails because it is itching.

scream screams, screaming, screamed

If you scream, you cry out loudly, often because you are hurt or afraid.

sea seas

The sea is the salt water that covers most of the Earth's surface.

seal seals

A seal is a furry animal that lives in the sea and on land. Seals have flippers for swimming.

search searches, searching, searched

When you search for something, you look very carefully for it.

seaside

The seaside is a place by the sea where people go for a holiday.

season seasons

A season is one of the four parts of the year. The four seasons are called spring, summer, autumn, and winter.

seat seats

A seat is anything that people sit on.

second

If you are second, you are the next one after the first.

secret secrets

A secret is something that you do not want other people to know about.

see sees, seeing, saw, seen

When you see, you use your eyes to get to know something.

seed seeds

A seed is a tiny part of the fruit of a plant. When a seed is put in the ground, it can grow into a new plant.

sell sells, selling, sold

If someone sells you something, they let you have it for some money.

send sends, sending, sent

If you send a person or thing, you make them go somewhere.

sensible

Sensible people are good at knowing what is best to do.

set sets

A set is a group of things that belong together.

set sets, setting, set

1 When something like glue or jelly sets, it becomes solid or hard.
2 When the sun sets, it goes down at the end of the day.

shadow shadows

A shadow is the dark shape that is made by something standing in front of the light.

shake shakes, shaking, shook, shaken

If you shake something, you move it quickly up and down or from side to side.

a
b
c
d
e
f
g
h
i
j
k
l
m
n
o
p
q
r
S
t
u
v
w
x
y
z

shallow shallower, shallowest

Something, like water, that is shallow is not deep.

shape shapes

The shape of something is the pattern that its outside edges make. Circles, squares, and triangles are all shapes.

share shares, sharing, shared

If you share something, you give some of it to other people.

shark sharks

A shark is a large sea fish with lots of sharp teeth.

sharp sharper, sharpest

Something sharp has an edge or point that can cut or make holes.

shave shaves, shaving, shaved

When people shave, they cut hair from their skin to make it smooth.

shed sheds

A shed is a small building made of wood. People often keep tools or bicycles in a shed.

sheep sheep

A sheep is an animal kept by farmers for its wool and meat.

sheet sheets

1 A sheet is one of the large pieces of cloth that you put on a bed.
2 A sheet is also a piece of paper or glass.

shelf shelves

A shelf is a long flat surface for putting things on. Bookcases and cupboards have shelves.

shell shells

A shell is the hard part on the outside of eggs, nuts, and some kinds of animals such as snails and tortoises.

shine shines, shining, shone

When something shines, it gives out light, or looks very bright.

shiny shinier, shiniest

When things are shiny, they look very bright.

ship ships

A ship is a large boat that takes people or things across the sea.

shirt shirts

You wear a shirt on the top half of your body. Shirts have sleeves, a collar, and buttons down the front.

shiver shivers, shivering, shivered

When you shiver, you shake because you are cold or frightened.

shoe shoes

A shoe is a strong covering for your foot.

shop shops

A shop is a place where people go to buy things.

short shorter, shortest

1 A short distance or time is not very long.
2 A short person is not very tall.

shorts

Shorts are short trousers that end above your knees.

shoulder shoulders

Your shoulder is the part of your body between your neck and the top of your arm.

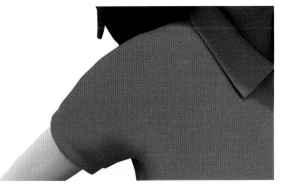

shout shouts, shouting, shouted

When you shout, you speak very loudly.

a
b
c
d
e
f
g
h
i
j
k
l
m
n
o
p
q
r
s
t
u
v
w
x
y
z

95

show shows, showing, showed, shown

1 When you show something, you let someone else see it.

2 If someone shows you how to do something, they do it so that you can watch them and learn how to do it.

show shows

A show is something that is put on for you to watch, like a television programme, a play, or dancing.

shower showers

1 A shower is rain or snow that falls for only a short time.

2 A shower in the bathroom gives you a spray of water so that you can stand under it and wash all over.

shut shuts, shutting, shut

To shut means to move a cover, lid, or door to close up an opening.

shy shyer, shyest

Someone who is shy is a bit nervous about talking to people they do not know.

sick

Someone who is sick does not feel well.

side sides

1 The side is the part that is on the left or right of something.

2 A side can be an edge. A triangle has three sides and a square has four sides.

3 A side can also be a flat surface. A dice has six sides.

4 The two sides in a game are the groups playing against each other.

sign signs

A sign is anything that is written, drawn, or done to tell or show people something.

sign signs, signing, signed

When you sign something, you write your name on it.

silent

A person or thing that is silent does not make any sound at all.

silly sillier, silliest

A silly person does something that is funny or not sensible.

silver

Silver is a valuable, shiny white metal.

sing sings, singing, sang, sung

When you sing, you make music with your voice.

sink sinks

A sink is a place where you can wash things.

sink sinks, sinking, sank, sunk

If something sinks, it goes downwards, usually under water.

sister sisters

Your sister is a girl who has the same parents as you do.

sit sits, sitting, sat

When you sit, you rest on your bottom on a chair or on the floor.

size sizes

The size of something is how big it is.

skate skates

An ice skate is a special boot with a sharp piece of metal fixed under it. A roller skate has small wheels instead.

skeleton skeletons

A skeleton is all the bones that hold up the body of a person or animal.

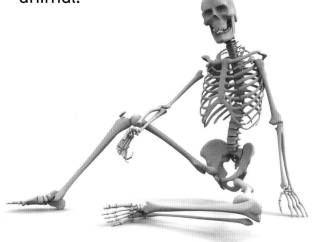

skin skins

1 Your skin covers the outside of your body.
2 The covering on the outside of fruit and vegetables is also called skin.

skirt skirts

A skirt is worn by women and girls. It hangs down from the waist.

A B C D E F G H I J K L M N O P Q R **S** T U V W X Y Z

sky skies

The sky is the space above the Earth where you can see the clouds, sun, moon, and stars.

sleep sleeps, sleeping, slept

When you sleep, you close your eyes and let your body rest as it does every night.

sleeve sleeves

A sleeve is the part of something like a coat or shirt that covers your arm.

slice slices

A slice of something like bread or cake is a thin piece cut from the whole thing.

slide slides, sliding, slid

If you slide, you move quickly over a smooth surface.

slide slides

A slide is a smooth slope that you can slide down for fun.

slip slips, slipping, slipped

If you slip, you slide suddenly without meaning to.

slipper slippers

Slippers are soft shoes that people wear indoors.

slope slopes

A slope is ground that is like the side of a hill, with one end lower than the other.

slow slower, slowest

Someone or something that is slow does not move very fast or takes a long time.

small smaller, smallest

Small things are not as big as others of the same kind.

smash smashes, smashing, smashed

If something smashes, it breaks into lots of pieces with a loud noise.

smell smells, smelling, smelt

1 When you smell something, you use your nose to find out about it.
2 When something smells, you can find out about it with your nose.

smile smiles, smiling, smiled

When you smile, your face shows that you are feeling happy.

smoke

Smoke is a grey or black cloud of gas that floats up from a fire.

smooth smoother, smoothest

Something that is smooth does not have any bumps or rough parts.

snail snails

A snail is a small, soft animal that lives inside a shell. Snails move very slowly.

snake snakes

A snake is an animal with a long, thin body and no legs.

sneeze sneezes, sneezing, sneezed

When you sneeze, you make a sudden noise as air blows out of your nose.

snow

Snow is small, white pieces of frozen water. It floats down from the sky when the weather is very cold.

snowman snowmen

A snowman is a shape of a person made out of snow.

soap

You use soap with water for washing. Soap can be solid, liquid, or a powder.

sock socks

A sock is a soft covering for your foot and part of your leg.

sofa sofas

A sofa is a long comfortable seat with a back, for more than one person.

a b c d e f g h i j k l m n o p q r **S** t u v w x y z

soft softer, softest
Something that is soft is not hard.

soil
Soil is the earth that plants grow in.

soldier soldiers
A soldier is a person in an army.

solid
1 Something that is solid does not have space inside.
2 Something that is solid does not change its shape. Liquids and gases are not solid, but rocks and metals are.

son sons
A person's son is their male child.

song songs
A song is words that are sung.

soon
Soon means in a short time.

sore sorer, sorest
If part of your body is sore, it hurts.

sorry
You say you are sorry when you have done something wrong.

sort sorts
If things are of the same sort, they belong to the same group or kind.

sort sorts, sorting, sorted
When you sort things, you put them into different groups.

sound sounds
A sound is anything you can hear.

soup
Soup is a liquid food made from vegetables or meat and water. You eat soup with a spoon out of a bowl.

sour
Things that are sour have the kind of taste a lemon or vinegar has.

space spaces
1 Space is an empty place where there is room for something.
2 Space is everything around and away from the Earth, where the stars and planets are.

spaceship spaceships
A spaceship is a vehicle that can carry people and things through space.

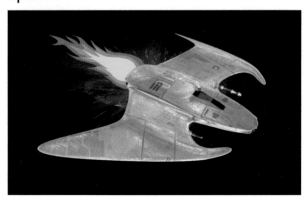

spade spades

A spade is a tool used for digging. It has a long handle and a wide, flat part at the end.

speak speaks, speaking, spoke, spoken

If you speak, you say something.

special

1 If something is special, it is better than the usual kind.
2 Special also means made for one job. For example, you need special shoes for tap dancing and special tools for making a clock.

speed speeds

Speed is how quickly something moves or happens.

spell spells, spelling, spelt, spelled

When you spell a word, you say or write the letters in the right order.

spell spells

In stories, a spell is words that make magic things happen.

spend spends, spending, spent

1 When you spend money, you use it to pay for things.
2 When you spend time, you use it to do something.

spider spiders

A spider is a small animal with eight legs. Many spiders make webs to catch insects to eat.

spill spills, spilling, spilt, spilled

If you spill a liquid, you let it flow out when you did not mean to.

spin spins, spinning, spun

To spin means to turn round and round quickly.

splash splashes, splashing, splashed

When liquid splashes, it flies about in drops.

spoil spoils, spoiling, spoilt, spoiled

If something is spoilt, it is not as good as it was before.

a b c d e f g h i j k l m n o p q r **S** t u v w x y z

spoon spoons

You use a spoon to eat things like soup, cereal, and puddings.

sport sports

A sport is a game that you play to get exercise and have fun. Football, tennis, and swimming are sports.

spot spots

1 A spot is a round mark.
2 A spot is also a small, red bump on your skin.
3 A spot can mean a place.

spout spouts

A spout is part of something like a jug, kettle, or teapot. It is made so that you can pour liquid out easily.

spring springs

1 Spring is the part of the year when plants start to grow and the days get longer and warmer.

2 A spring is a curly piece of metal. It jumps back into shape after you press it down or stretch it.

square squares

A square is a shape with four corners and four equal sides.

squirrel squirrels

A squirrel is a small wild animal with a long, thick tail. Squirrels live in trees and eat nuts.

stable stables

A stable is a building where horses are kept.

stair stairs

Stairs are the set of steps for going up or down inside a building.

stamp stamps

A stamp is a small piece of paper that you stick on an envelope or parcel before you post it.

stand stands, standing, stood

When you stand, you are on your feet without moving.

star stars

1 A star is one of the tiny, bright lights you see in the sky at night.

2 A star is also somebody famous, like a singer or actor.

start starts, starting, started

When you start, you take the first steps in doing something.

station stations

1 A station is a place where you can catch a train.
2 A station is also a building where the police or firefighters work.

stay stays, staying, stayed

1 If you stay somewhere, you do not move away from there.
2 If you stay with someone, you live with them for a little while.

steady steadier, steadiest

Something that is steady is not shaking at all.

steal steals, stealing, stole, stolen

To steal is to take something that belongs to someone else.

steam

Steam is very hot water that has turned into a cloud.

steel

Steel is a strong, shiny metal.

steep steeper, steepest

If a slope is steep, it is hard to climb.

stem stems

A stem is the main part of a plant above the ground. A stem holds a flower or leaf or fruit to the rest of the plant.

step steps

1 When you take a step, you move your foot as you are walking, running, or dancing.
2 A step is also a flat place where you can put your foot when you are going up or down stairs or a ladder.

stick sticks

A stick is a long, thin piece of wood.

a
b
c
d
e
f
g
h
i
j
k
l
m
n
o
p
q
r
S
t
u
v
w
x
y
z

stick sticks, sticking, stuck

1 If something sticks to something else, it becomes fixed to it.

2 If you stick something sharp into a thing, you push the point in.

stiff stiffer, stiffest

Something that is stiff is not easy to bend.

still

Still means not moving at all.

sting stings, stinging, stung

If something stings you, it hurts you with the sharp point it has. Bees can sting you.

stir stirs, stirring, stirred

When you stir a liquid or a soft mixture, you move it around with a spoon or a stick.

stomach stomachs

Your stomach is the part of your body where your food goes after you swallow it.

stone stones

1 A stone is a small piece of rock.

2 A stone is also the hard seed in the middle of some fruits.

stop stops, stopping, stopped

1 If a person or thing stops doing something, they do not do it any more.

2 If something that is moving stops, it comes to rest.

store stores, storing, stored

If you store something, you keep it until it is needed.

storm storms

A storm is very bad weather with strong wind and a lot of rain. There is sometimes thunder and lightning too.

story stories

A story tells you about something that has happened. A story can be made up, or it can be real.

straight straighter, straightest

Something that is straight has no bends or curves in it.

strange stranger, strangest

If something is strange, it is not like anything you have seen or heard before.

A B C D E F G H I J K L M N O P Q R **S** T U V W X Y Z

straw straws

1 Straw is the dry stems of corn and wheat.

2 A straw is a very thin tube for drinking through.

stream streams

A stream is a small river.

street streets

A street is a road with houses and other buildings along each side.

stretch stretches, stretching, stretched

When you stretch something, you pull it to make it longer, wider, or tighter.

strict stricter, strictest

When someone is strict, they make people do what they say and obey the rules.

string

String is very thin rope.

stripe stripes

A stripe is a thin band of colour. Tigers have stripes on their bodies, and so do zebras.

strong stronger, strongest

1 Strong people or animals are healthy and can carry heavy things and work hard.

2 Something strong is hard to break or damage.

3 Food or drink that is strong has a lot of flavour.

submarine submarines

A submarine is a ship that can travel under water as well as on the surface.

suck sucks, sucking, sucked

If you suck something, you draw liquid from it into your mouth.

sudden

Things that are sudden happen quickly when you do not expect them.

suddenly

If something happens suddenly, it happens quickly without any warning.

sugar

Sugar is used to put in foods and drinks to make them taste sweet.

a
b
c
d
e
f
g
h
i
j
k
l
m
n
o
p
q
r
s
t
u
v
w
x
y
z

sum sums

A sum is a problem that you work out using numbers.

summer summers

Summer is the hottest season of the year.

sun

The sun gives the Earth heat and light. It is a star, and the Earth moves round it.

sunny sunnier, sunniest

It is a sunny day when the sun is shining.

supermarket supermarkets

A supermarket is a big shop that sells food and other things. People help themselves to things as they go round, and pay for them on the way out.

sure surer, surest

If you are sure about something, you believe it is true or right.

surface surfaces

The surface of a thing is the top or outside part of it.

surprise surprises

A surprise is something that you did not expect.

swallow swallows, swallowing, swallowed

When you swallow something, you make it go down your throat and into your stomach.

swan swans

A swan is a large, white bird with a long, curved neck. Swans live by rivers and lakes.

sweep sweeps, sweeping, swept

When you sweep, you use a broom to clear away dust and litter.

sweet sweeter, sweetest
Sweet things have the taste of sugar.

swim swims, swimming, swam, swum
When you swim, you move your body through water using your arms and legs.

swing swings, swinging, swung
When something swings, it moves backwards and forwards in the air.

switch switches
A switch is anything that you turn or press to start or stop something working.

sword swords
People fought with swords in the past. A sword has a handle and a long, sharp edge.

Tt

table tables
A table is a piece of furniture. It has legs and a flat top.

tadpole tadpoles
Tadpoles are tiny animals that live in water. They grow into frogs.

tail tails
An animal's tail is the part that grows out from the back end of its body.

take takes, taking, took, taken
1 When you take something, you get it in your hands.
2 Take also means to bring or carry something.

talk talks, talking, talked
When you talk, you speak to other people.

tall taller, tallest
A tall person or thing measures more than usual from top to bottom.

tame tamer, tamest

Tame animals are friendly to humans and not afraid of them.

tap taps

A tap lets you turn water on and off.

tape tapes

Tape is a long, narrow piece of paper or plastic with a sticky back. You can use tape for sticking things together.

taste tastes

The taste of something is what it is like when you eat or drink it.

taste tastes, tasting, tasted

When you taste something, you eat or drink a bit of it to see what it is like.

tea teas

Tea is a hot drink, made with boiling water and the leaves of tea plants.

teach teaches, teaching, taught

When someone teaches, they help people to understand something, or show them how to do it.

teacher teachers

A teacher is someone whose job is to teach.

team teams

A team is a group of people who work together, or who play together on the same side.

tear tears

A tear is a drop of water that falls from your eye when you cry.

tear tears, tearing, tore, torn

If you tear something, you pull it apart.

telephone telephones

You use a telephone to speak to someone far away.

television televisions

A television is a machine that picks up sounds and pictures sent through the air.

tell tells, telling, told

1 If somebody tells you something, they pass on news or information or a story.
2 If someone tells you to do something, they say you must do it.

tent tents

A tent is made of strong cloth stretched over poles. You can sleep in a tent when you go camping.

term terms

A term is part of a school year. It is the time in between the holidays, when the school is open.

test tests

A test is something you do to show how much you know.

thank thanks, thanking, thanked

You thank someone when they have done something for you or given you something.

theatre theatres

A theatre is a place where you go to see plays and shows.

thick thicker, thickest

1 Something that is thick measures a lot from one side to the other.

2 Thick liquids do not flow easily.

thin thinner, thinnest

1 A thin person or animal does not weigh very much.

2 Something that is thin does not measure much from one side to the other.

think thinks, thinking, thought

When you think, you use your mind to work something out.

thirsty thirstier, thirstiest

If you are thirsty, you need a drink.

throat throats

Your throat is the front part of your neck, and the tubes inside that take food, drink, and air into your body.

throw throws, throwing, threw, thrown

When you throw something, you make it leave your hand and move through the air.

thumb thumbs

Your thumb is the short, thick finger at the side of your hand.

thunder

Thunder is the loud noise that follows a flash of lightning in a storm.

tidy tidier, tidiest
If something is tidy, everything is in the right place and it is not in a mess.

tie ties
1 A tie is a long piece of material that is worn around the collar of a shirt and hangs down the front.
2 When two people do as well as each other in a race or have the same score in a game, it is called a tie.

tie ties, tying, tied
When you tie something, you make a knot.

tiger tigers
A tiger is a big wild cat found in India and China. It has orange fur with black stripes.

tight tighter, tightest
If something is tight, it fits closely or is fixed firmly.

time
1 Time is how long something takes. It is measured in minutes, hours, days, and years.
2 The time is the hour and minutes when something is happening. You tell the time by looking at a clock or watch.

tin tins
You can buy food in round metal tins.

tiny tinier, tiniest
Tiny things are very small.

tired
When you are tired, you need to rest or sleep.

today
Today means on this day.

toe toes
Your toes are the five parts at the end of each of your feet.

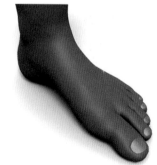

tomorrow
Tomorrow means on the day after today.

tongue tongues
Your tongue is the long, soft, pink part that you move inside your mouth.

tonight
Tonight means the night at the end of today.

tool tools
A tool is something that you use in your hand to help you do a job. Hammers and saws are tools.

tooth teeth
A tooth is one of the hard, white parts in your mouth.

top tops
1 The top of something is the highest part.
2 The top is the part that covers something like a jar, tube, or pen.

touch touches, touching, touched
1 If you touch something, you put your hand or fingers on it.
2 If things are touching, they are so close there is no space between them.

towel towels
A towel is a piece of cloth to dry yourself with.

town towns
A town is a place with a lot of houses, shops, and other buildings.

toy toys
A toy is something you play with.

tractor tractors
A tractor is a vehicle with a strong engine used for pulling heavy things on a farm.

traffic
Traffic is all the cars, buses, lorries, and other things travelling on the road.

train trains
A train carries people or things on railway lines.

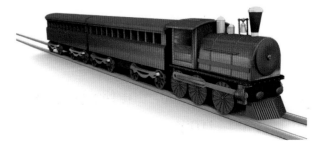

a
b
c
d
e
f
g
h
i
j
k
l
m
n
o
p
q
r
s
t
u
v
w
x
y
z

111

A B C D E F G H I J K L M N O P Q R S **T** U V W X Y Z

travel travels, travelling, travelled

When you travel, you go on a journey.

tree trees

A tree is any tall plant with leaves, branches, and a thick stem of wood, called a trunk.

triangle triangles

A triangle is a shape with three straight sides and three points.

trick tricks

A trick is a clever thing that you have learned to do.

trousers

Trousers cover each leg and the lower part of your body.

truck trucks

A truck is a kind of large vehicle that is used to carry things from place to place.

true truer, truest

1 If a story is true, it really happened.
2 Something that is true is right.

trunk trunks

1 A trunk is the thick stem of a tree from which the branches grow.
2 An elephant's trunk is its long nose.

try tries, trying, tried

If you try to do something, you see if you can do it.

tube tubes

1 Tubes are used to hold soft mixtures such as toothpaste.
2 A tube is also a kind of pipe.

tunnel tunnels

A tunnel is a long hole under the ground or through a hill.

turn turns, turning, turned

1 When you turn, you move round or change direction.
2 When something turns into something else, it changes.

Uu

turn turns

If it is your turn, it is time for you to do something.

tusk tusks

A tusk is one of the two long, pointed teeth that elephants have next to their trunk.

twin twins

Twins are two children who have the same parents and were born at the same time.

twist twists, twisting, twisted

1 When you twist something, you turn or bend it.
2 To twist also means to wrap things around each other.

tyre tyres

A tyre is a circle of rubber that goes round the edge of a wheel.

ugly uglier, ugliest

People and things that are ugly are not nice to look at.

umbrella umbrellas

An umbrella is cloth stretched over a frame, which you hold over your head to keep off the rain.

uncle uncles

Your uncle is the brother of your mother or father, or the husband of your aunt.

understand understands, understanding, understood

If you understand something, you know what it means or how it works.

a
b
c
d
e
f
g
h
i
j
k
l
m
n
o
p
q
r
s
t
u
v
w
x
y
z

113

undress undresses, undressing, undressed

When you undress, you take your clothes off.

uniform uniforms

A uniform is a special set of clothes people wear to show which school they go to or what job they do.

upset

If you are upset, you are sad or crying.

upside down

When something is upside down, the bottom part is at the top.

use uses, using, used

When you use something, you do a job with it.

useful

Something that is useful can be used to help you in some way.

usual

Something that is usual is what happens most times.

Vv

valley valleys

A valley is the low land between hills or mountains.

valuable

You could sell something valuable for a lot of money.

van vans

A van is a covered vehicle for carrying things and people.

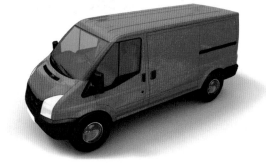

vase vases

A vase is used for holding flowers.

vegetable vegetables

A vegetable is part of a plant that is used as food.

vehicle vehicles

A vehicle is anything that takes people and things from place to place. Cars, trucks, and bicycles are vehicles.

vet vets

A vet is a person whose job is to take care of sick animals.

village villages

A village is a group of houses together with other buildings in the country. A village is smaller than a town.

visit visits, visiting, visited

When you visit someone, you go to see them.

voice voices

Your voice is the sound you make when you are speaking or singing.

volcano volcanoes

A volcano is a mountain that sometimes has hot, melted rock and smoke bursting out of it.

Ww

wait waits, waiting, waited

If you wait, you stay for something that you are expecting to happen.

wake wakes, waking, woke, woken

When you wake up, you stop sleeping.

walk walks, walking, walked

When you walk, you move along by putting one foot in front of the other.

wall walls

1 A wall is any one of the sides of a building or room.
2 Walls made of brick or stone are also used round fields and gardens.

want wants, wanting, wanted

When you want something, you feel that you would like it.

a
b
c
d
e
f
g
h
i
j
k
l
m
n
o
p
q
r
s
t
u
v
w
x
y
z

warm warmer, warmest

If something is warm, it feels quite hot but not too hot.

warn warns, warning, warned

If you warn someone, you tell them that there is danger.

wash washes, washing, washed

When you wash something, you make it clean with water and soap.

wasp wasps

A wasp is a flying insect with black and yellow stripes. It has a sting.

waste wastes, wasting, wasted

If you waste something, you use more of it than you need.

watch watches, watching, watched

If you watch something, you look to see what happens.

watch watches

A watch is a small clock that you wear on your wrist.

water

Water is the liquid in rivers and seas. It falls from the sky as rain.

wave waves, waving, waved

If you wave, you move your hand about in the air.

wave waves

Waves are moving lines of water on the surface of the sea.

wax

Wax is used to make things like candles and crayons. It is soft and melts easily.

way ways

1 The way to a place is how to get there.
2 The way to do something is how to do it.

weak weaker, weakest
People or things that are weak are not strong.

wear wears, wearing, wore, worn
1 When you wear something, you are dressed in it.
2 When something wears out, it becomes so old that you cannot use it any more.

weather
The weather is how it is outside, for example sunny or raining.

web webs
A web is a thin, sticky net made by a spider to catch insects. It is also called a cobweb.

week weeks
A week is seven days. There are fifty-two weeks in a year.

weigh weighs, weighing, weighed
When you weigh something, you find out how heavy it is.

well better, best
1 If you do something well, you are good at it, or make a good job of it.
2 If you are well, you are healthy.

wet wetter, wettest
If something is wet, it is covered in water, or has water in it.

whale whales
A whale is a very large sea animal. It breathes through a hole in the top of its head.

wheat
Wheat is a plant grown by farmers. Its seed is used for making flour.

wheel wheels
Wheels are round and they turn. Cars and bicycles move along on wheels.

wheelchair wheelchairs
A wheelchair is a chair that moves on wheels. It is used by people who cannot walk.

whisper whispers, whispering, whispered

When you whisper, you speak very quietly.

whistle whistles, whistling, whistled

When you whistle, you make a loud, high sound by blowing air through your lips.

whistle whistles

A whistle is a small tube that makes a loud, high sound when you blow it.

whole

Whole means all of something, with nothing missing.

wide wider, widest

Something that is wide measures a lot from side to side.

wild wilder, wildest

Wild animals and plants live and grow without people looking after them.

win wins, winning, won

When you win, you beat everybody else in a game or race.

wind winds

Wind is air moving along quickly.

window windows

A window is an opening in the wall of a building, or in a vehicle. Windows are for letting in light and air. Most windows have glass in them.

wing wings

A wing is one of the parts of a bird or insect that it uses for flying. An aeroplane also has wings.

winter winters

Winter is the coldest part of the year.

wire wires

A wire is a long, thin piece of metal that can be bent easily.

wish wishes, wishing, wished

When you wish, you say or think what you would like to happen.

witch witches

In stories, a witch is a woman who can do magic.

wizard wizards

In stories, a wizard is a man who can do magic.

woman women

A woman is a grown-up female person.

wood woods

1 Wood is what trees are made of. It can be used to make things like furniture and paper.
2 A wood is a lot of trees growing together.

wool

Wool is the thick, soft hair that covers sheep. It is used for making clothes.

word words

You use words when you speak or write. Words that are written have a space on each side.

work

Work is a job or something that you have to do.

work works, working, worked

1 If a machine works, it does what it is meant to do.
2 When you work, you do a job or try hard to do something.

world worlds

The world is the Earth and everything on it.

worm worms

A worm is a small animal with a long, thin body and no legs. Worms live in the ground.

worry worries, worrying, worried

When you worry, you keep thinking about something bad that might happen.

worse

If one thing is worse than another, it is not as good.

a
b
c
d
e
f
g
h
i
j
k
l
m
n
o
p
q
r
s
t
u
v
w
x
y
z

worst

Worst means so bad that none of the others are as bad as that.

wrap wraps, wrapping, wrapped

When you wrap something, you cover it in something like paper or cloth.

wrist wrists

Your wrist is the thin part of your arm where it joins your hand.

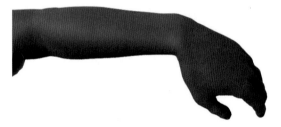

write writes, writing, wrote, written

When you write, you put words on paper so that people can read them.

wrong

Something that is wrong is not right.

X-ray X-rays

An X-ray is a special photograph that shows the inside of a body.

yacht yachts

A yacht is a boat with sails.

yawn yawns, yawning, yawned

When you yawn, you open your mouth wide and take in a lot of air. You yawn when you are tired or bored.

year years

A year is a measure of time. There are twelve months in a year.

yesterday

Yesterday means on the day before today.

yogurt yogurts

Yogurt or yoghurt is a food made from milk. It tastes a little sour and often has fruit in it.

young younger, youngest

A person or animal that is young was born not long ago.

Zz

zebra zebras

A zebra is an animal that looks like a horse with black and white stripes. Zebras live in Africa.

zip zips

A zip is used to fasten two edges of material together. Some dresses, trousers, and bags have zips.

zoo zoos

A zoo is a place where different kinds of wild animal are kept so that people can go and look at them.

a b c d e f g h i j k l m n o p q r s t u v w x y z

121

The alphabet

Aa apple

Bb ball

Cc caterpillar

Dd dinosaur

Ee elephant

Ff fish

Gg guitar

Hh helicopter

Ii ink

Jj jigsaw

Kk kangaroo

Ll lion

Mm mouse

Nn number

Oo octopus

Pp parrot

Qq queen

Rr rocket

Ss sock

Tt tiger

Uu umbrella

Vv van

Ww watch

Xx X-ray

Yy yacht

Zz zebra

ch cheese

sh ship

th thumb

wh whistle

How many words can you think of beginning with the letter **o**?

Numbers

0	zero	
1	one	■
2	two	■■
3	three	■■■
4	four	■■■■
5	five	■■■■■
6	six	■■■■■■
7	seven	■■■■■■■
8	eight	■■■■■■■■
9	nine	■■■■■■■■■
10	ten	■■■■■■■■■■
11	eleven	■■■■■■■■■■■
12	twelve	■■■■■■■■■■■■
13	thirteen	■■■■■■■■■■■■■
14	fourteen	■■■■■■■■■■■■■■
15	fifteen	■■■■■■■■■■■■■■■
16	sixteen	■■■■■■■■■■■■■■■■
17	seventeen	■■■■■■■■■■■■■■■■■
18	eighteen	■■■■■■■■■■■■■■■■■■
19	nineteen	■■■■■■■■■■■■■■■■■■■
20	twenty	■■■■■■■■■■■■■■■■■■■■

What is
9 + 10 = ?

123

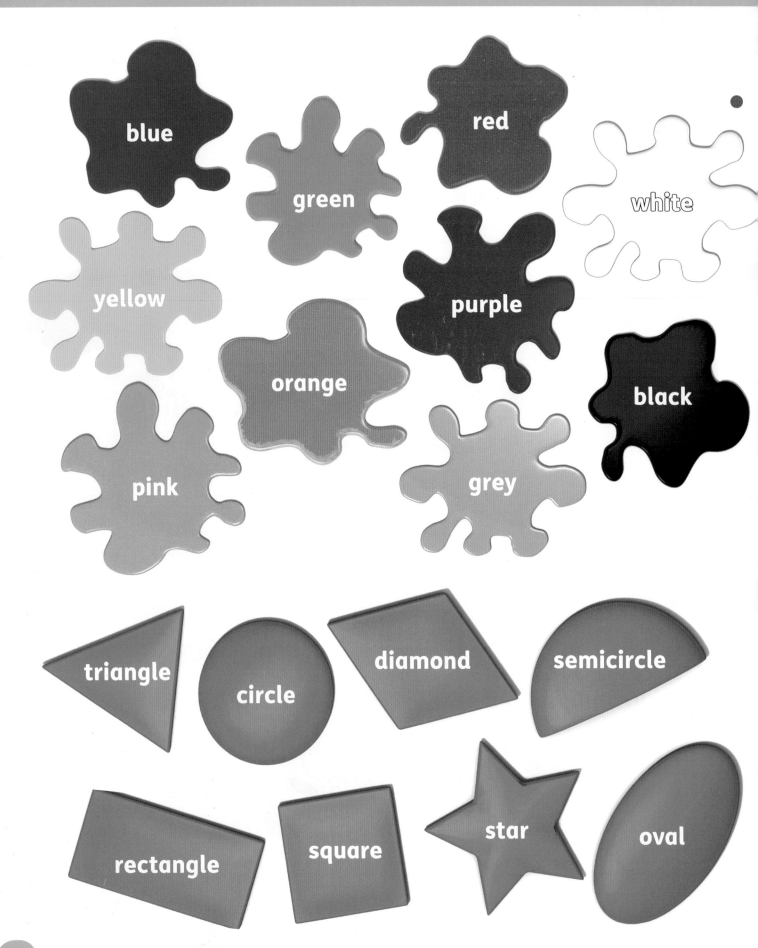

blue

green

red

white

yellow

purple

orange

black

pink

grey

triangle

circle

diamond

semicircle

rectangle

square

star

oval

Time

9:00
nine o'clock

3:15
quarter past three

12:30
half past twelve

2:45
quarter to three

Days and months

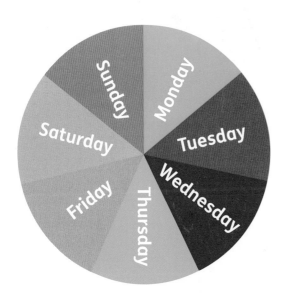

Sunday
Monday
Saturday
Tuesday
Wednesday
Friday
Thursday

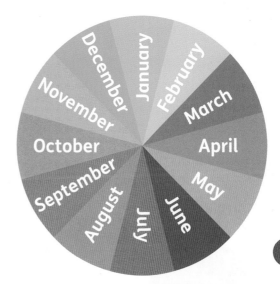

December
January
November
February
October
March
April
September
May
August
July
June

Seasons

winter

spring

summer

autumn

125

eyebrow

forehead

ear

hair

eye

nose

cheek

chin

neck

mouth

finger

thumb

hand

wrist

arm

shoulder

elbow

stomach

heel

toe

knee

ankle

leg

foot

Question words

when   where   which

what   who   why

Words we use in stories

beginning   once upon a time

one day   happy   end

Words we use a lot

a about after again all am an and any are as at away

be because been but by

can could

down

every everyone

for from

he her hers here him his how

I if in inside into is it

me mine more much my

no not

of off on once only or other our ours out outside over

put

she should so some

than that the their theirs them then there these they this those to too

up us

very

was we were will with would

yes you your yours

What is the difference between a wet day and a lion with a toothache?

One pours with rain and the other roars with pain.

What did the little candle say to the big candle?

I am going out tonight.

What did one ear say to the other ear?

Between you and me, we need a haircut.

What did the stamp say to the envelope?

Stick with me and we will go places.

What is the crocodile's favourite game?

Snap.

How do you start a teddy bear race?

Ready, teddy, go!